Constellations of the Caucasus

Constellations of the Caucasus

Empires, Peoples, and Faiths

Michael A. Reynolds
Editor

Markus Wiener Publishers
Princeton

Copyright © 2016 by the Department of Near Eastern Studies, Princeton University.

Reprinted from *Princeton Papers: Interdisciplinary Journal of Middle Eastern Studies*, Volume XVII.

All rights reserved. No part of this book may be reproduced or transmitted in any form or by any means, whether electronic or mechanical—including photocopying or recording—or through any information storage or retrieval system, without permission of the copyright owners.

For information write to: Markus Wiener Publishers
231 Nassau Street, Princeton, NJ 08542
www.markuswiener.com

Library of Congress Cataloging-in-Publication Data

Names: Reynolds, Michael A., 1968- editor. | Pollock, Sean, 1970- author. | Maeda, Hirotake, 1971- author. | Suny, Ronald Grigor, author. | Kemper, Michael, author. | Shikhaliev, Sh. Sh., author.
Title: Constellations of the Caucasus : empires, peoples, and faiths / Michael A. Reynolds, editor ; Sean Pollock, Hirotake Maeda, Ronald Gregor Suny, Michael Kemper and Shamil Shikhaliev.
Description: Princeton, New Jersey : Markus Wiener Publishers, 2016. | Includes bibliographical references.
Identifiers: LCCN 2015043805
  ISBN 9781558766044 (hardcover)
  ISBN 9781558766051 (paperback)
Subjects: LCSH: Caucasus, South--History. | Caucasus, South--Civilization. | Caucasus, South—Religion. | Caucasus, Northern (Russia)—History. | Caucasus, Northern (Russia)—Civilization. | Caucasus, Northern (Russia)—Religion.
Classification: LCC DK509 .C65 2016 | DDC 947.5--dc23
LC record available at http://lccn.loc.gov/2015043805

Markus Wiener Publishers books are printed in the United States of America on acid-free paper, and meet the guidelines for permanence and durability of the Committee on Production Guidelines for Book Longevity of the Council on Library Resources.

Contents

List of Maps vi

List of Figures and Illustrations vii

MICHAEL A. REYNOLDS
Constellations of the Caucasus: Introduction 1

SEAN POLLOCK
Friend and Foe: Religious Toleration in Northern Caucasia
in the Age of Catherine the Great 25

HIROTAKE MAEDA
Transcending Boundaries: When the Mamluk Legacy
Meets a Family of Armeno-Georgian Interpreters 63

RONALD GRIGOR SUNY
Effects of Empire: Tsarism as Enabler and Constraint
on the Peoples of Caucasia 87

MICHAEL KEMPER and SHAMIL SHIKHALIEV
Islam and Political Violence in Post-Soviet Daghestan:
Discursive Strategies of the Sufi Masters 117

About the Editor and Contributors 155

List of Maps

Map 1: Topographic Map of the Caucasus viii

Map 2: The Caucasus circa 1800 24

Map 3: The Caucasus in 1903 86

Map 4: The Caucasus Today 116

List of Figures and Illustrations

Figures
Aleksei Obreskov's Map of Northern Caucasia, 1764 39

Illustrations
Tomb in the valley of Pshat 4

Ossetian village 11

Mosque at Yerevan 17

Lezgin 27

Chechen Women 36

Circassian 44

Vladikavkaz, at the foot of the Caucasus 54

Bridge at Yerevan 65

An Armenian and a Georgian 72

Mingrelian Wine Jar 78

Echmiadzin Cathedral 90

Oil gusher outside Baku 99

Tiflis 110

Sayfallah-Qadi Bashlarov (1853–1919) 121

Said-Afandi from Chirkei (1937–2012) in the 1980s 124

Magomed-Saiid Saidov (1902–1985) in the manuscript section of the Institute of History, Archeology and Ethnography, 1970s. 130

Mahmudiyya masters, probably in the early 1980s 140

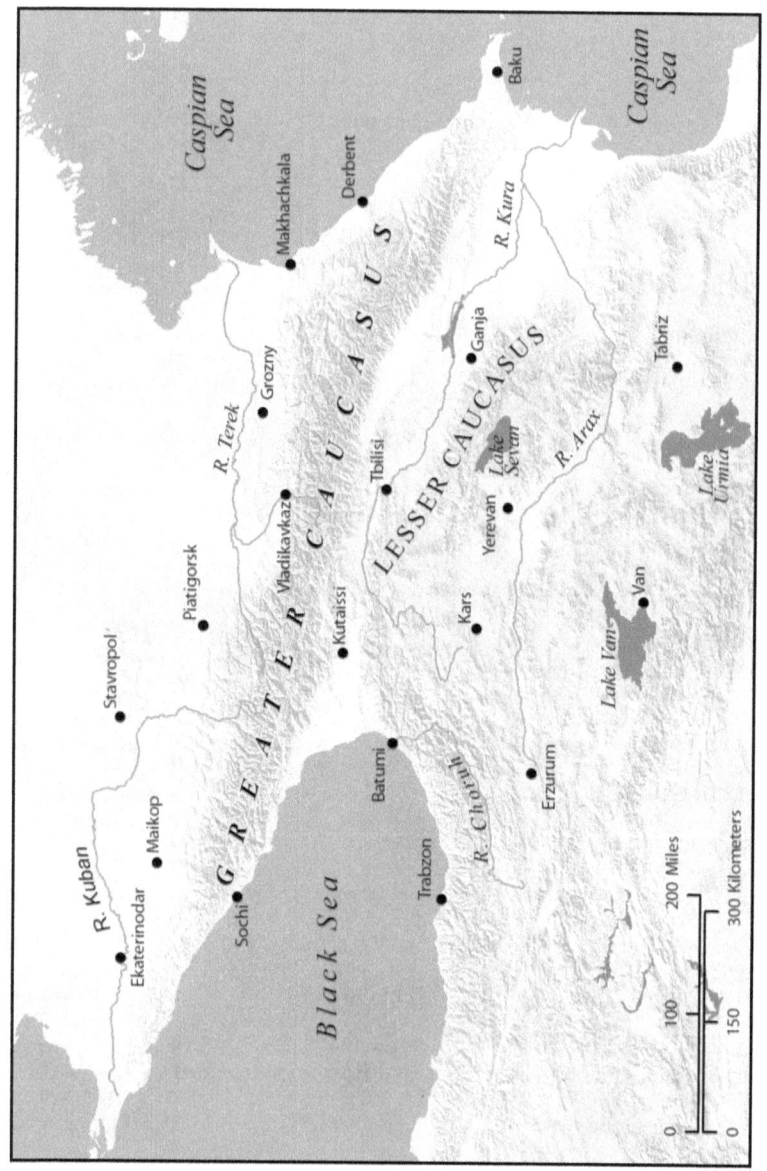

Topographic Map of the Caucasus

Constellations of the Caucasus: Introduction

MICHAEL A. REYNOLDS

Since antiquity, geographers, historians, and other scholars have recognized the Caucasus as a distinct—and distinctive—region. In part, this is a function of topography. A pair of mountain ranges defines the region. Stretching some 1,200 km northwest to southeast from the Taman Peninsula to the Apsheron Peninsula, the Greater Caucasus mountain range dominates the stretch of land that lies between the Black and Caspian Seas. Running parallel to this range and roughly one hundred kilometers to the south is the Lesser Caucasus mountain range. With its highest peak, Mt. Elbrus, reaching a height of 5,642 meters, the Greater Caucasus has loomed as a formidable barrier to communication north and south. Until the nineteenth century, the only pass through the Caucasus suitable for more than packhorses was the one that ran along the narrow Caspian shoreline. It is therefore not surprising that as early as the eighth century BC a fortress and city emerged at the narrowest point of this pass. Known today as Derbent, this city acquired its name from the Persian *Darband*, meaning "locked gate," an indicator of its key position along the route that connected the vast steppes of Eurasia with the Iranian plateau. Others also acknowledged the city's role in their nomenclature. The Arab-Muslim conquerors of the seventh century AD dubbed the city the *Bab al-Abwab*, "the Gate of Gates," and among Turkic peoples it came to be known as *Demirkapı*, "the Iron Gate."

On the western side of the Caucasus, the narrow and rocky eastern shore of the Black Sea offers no similarly traversable path. Thus, the only other significant pass across the Caucasus was through the Darial Gorge, located at an elevation of 1,800 meters in the western Caucasus where the Terek River skirts Mount Kazbek. Its name, like Derbent's, derives from Persian, *Dar-e Alan*, the "Gate of the Alans," or, as the Alans are known today, the Ossetians. Only at the beginning of the nineteenth century, when the Imperial Russian Army built the so-called "Georgian Military Highway" through the Darial Gorge to link the north and south Caucasus, did this route become capable of sustaining regular wheeled traffic. The increase in the flow of people and goods that the Georgian Military Highway made possible contributed to the rapid political and economic transformation of the South Caucasus under Imperial Russian rule.

The obstacles the Caucasus poses to human movement are not limited to high peaks and ridges. The poor navigability of its rivers means that its watercourses also often serve to hamper, not facilitate, communication. The Caucasus thus has throughout human history functioned as a massive geographic barrier impeding human travel and communication. Indeed, it is identified as a dividing line between the continents of Europe and Asia. It has repeatedly served to check imperial expansion and mark the space where imperial authority dissipates and runs out. The Roman and Byzantine, Sassanid, Arab Muslim (Caliphal), Khazar, Ilkhanid, Seljuk, Ottoman, and Safavid empires are just some of those whose borders ended at the Caucasus. Unified rule of the whole of the Caucasus came only in the second half of the nineteenth century under Imperial Russia. The disintegration of that rule in the Caucasus followed right on the heels of the fall of the tsar in March 1917, but by 1921 the Bolsheviks effectively brought the region under unified, central control. The collapse of the Soviet Union seven decades later in 1991, however, saw the Caucasus revert to a fractured state, as Georgia, Armenia, and Azerbaijan all asserted their sovereign status, and violent conflicts over borders and sovereignty marked the north as well as south.

Due to the same reason of geography, the Caucasus has never hosted an imperial metropole. Mountainous lands offer refuge to humans in flight, but they lack sufficient resources, such as arable land, to sustain large or dense populations. Moreover, the same factors that disrupt and impede outsiders' travel and communication across the region work also against the locals, thus keeping them divided and compelling (or enabling) them to live autonomously in small units. This is particularly true of the North Caucasus, but it holds true in the South as well. In the South Caucasus, the three major population groups—the Georgians, Armenians, and the Azerbaijanis—have at various times formed and sustained unitary polities but they have never unified the Caucasus nor established an empire. The Caucasus and its inhabitants, in other words, have repeatedly found themselves on the periphery of empires, but never at the center.[1]

The Caucasus, however, has stood out in human history for more than its forbidding and stunningly beautiful landscape. No less than the stunning physical geography of the Caucasus, the peoples and cultures of the region have fascinated outsiders and visitors for millennia. It has figured prominently as a place in mythology, as a repository of myths from different corners of the world, and as a source of new myths that were spread outward.[2] Most famously for Westerners, the Caucasus in the myths of the ancient Greeks was the site of the mountain where Prometheus was chained and the land where Jason and his Argonauts sought the Golden Fleece.[3] In the Turkic languages, the Caucasus Mountain, or *Kaf Dağı*, appears in fables and legends as a quasi-magical place inhabited by fairies and spirits. Turkic mystics suggest that the "Qaf chapter" of the Quran is an esoteric reference to the *Kaf Dağı*.[4]

The same disruption of communication and travel caused by the ridges, highlands, and rivers of the Caucasus impeded ethno-cultural homogenization and thereby fostered within the region the emergence of an extraordinary variety of languages and ethnicities. The dizzying array of peoples and tongues astounded the Arabs who attempted in vain to conquer the region. They dubbed the region *Jabal al-Lisan*, the "Mountain of Languages." This exceptional ethno-linguistic diversity continues to distinguish the Caucasus and intrigue researchers to the present day. The physical beauty and gracefulness of the Circassians, male and female alike, also left an impression upon the Arabs, and this, too, has been a long-lived trope of the Caucasus. The Ottomans prized Circassian women for their harems, and from them the legend of the "Circassian beauty" spread throughout the world, including to North America and Hollywood.[5] Indeed, the small peoples of the Caucasus have often exerted an outsize effect on popular

Tomb in the valley of Pshat

imaginations. Their customs, dress, and social relations regularly provoked interest. As will be discussed below, the Caucasus and its peoples figured prominently in Russian literature in the nineteenth century and in the formative debates on Russian identity and empire that unfolded in that literature. British, French, German, and other European authors testified to the unusual allure of the region's peoples.

The Caucasus, thus, has figured throughout human history as a distinctive region of human geography as well as of physical geography. This is despite the fact that it has never hosted an imperial center and has, more often than not, existed as a divided borderland on the peripheries of multiple empires. Nonetheless, the region and its peoples reemerge insistently as subjects of history and objects of historical interest.

Constellations

This raises a question. The Caucasus and its peoples have long attracted attention and clearly merit investigation. But how does one conceptualize the peoples and societies of a region where the inhabitants are fractured among themselves spatially, linguistically, religiously, and politically, and yet interact regularly with each other and with peoples in the surrounding regions? The usual boundary markers for historical subjects as state, ethnicity, tribe, or religion simply do not work well in the Caucasus. Up until perhaps the post-Soviet period, state could never have sufficed as a unit of analysis to discuss, even in general terms, the history and politics of the Caucasus. Although the terms of "tribe" and "clan" might be appropriate in some local contexts, the fact of the tremendous variation in the nature, functioning, and meaning of clan ties among the communities of the Caucasus swiftly attenuates their utility. Among just the North Caucasian highlanders one finds social relations that range from the complex hierarchy of the Kabardins to the expressly egalitarian structure of the Vainakh. In other words, tribe and clan in the Caucasus are too dependent on local context to serve as organizing concepts or even descriptive terms. Religion, too, cannot take one very far. Although one can, of course, divide the vast bulk of the region's inhabitants into Christians and Muslims, one sees the utility of the categories rapidly dissolve upon a closer look. Beyond the doctrinal fault lines separating Eastern Orthodox from Armenian Apostolic Christians and Sunni from Shi'i Muslims, one sees further divisions of practice and interpretation between Georgian and North Ossetian Christians and Avar and Adyghe Muslims. In the Caucasus, the standard categories of identity too often reveal themselves to be too diffuse for historical narrative and analysis.[6]

An alternative to these categories might be to apply the idea of "constellations." According to the Merriam-Webster Dictionary, a constellation is "an assemblage, collection, or group of usually related persons, qualities, or things, an assemblage of similar entities."[7] Constellation does not imply uniformity among its components. Similarity or relatedness suffices. Constellations are not exclusive. An entity's membership in one constellation has no logical or necessary bearing, for or against, its membership in others. Constellations thus can accommodate cleavages, both crosscutting and reinforcing ones. Constellations are not fixed or permanent. They can change, yet they are not evanescent. They therefore offer both stability and flexibility. Finally, the space of a constellation is not uniform and can accommodate different shapes. A constellation need not have a center and periphery. In short, the concept of constellation can help capture the social complexity of a variegated borderland like the Caucasus.

Of Bondage and Bonds

Whereas in the modern and contemporary eras the categories of state and nation constitute the most common subjects of history writing, in earlier periods dynasties often served as a basic unit for ordering politics. Among the perennial challenges facing dynastic rulers was that of maintaining the loyalty and obedience of the palace elites and of the warrior classes in particular. The latter groups sometimes concluded that they had less need of the ruler than the ruler had of them. One way that dynasties in the Muslim world sought to perpetuate their rule was through the acquisition and employment of slaves, young males in particular. These slave soldiers were commonly known as *mamluks* from the Arabic for "thing possessed," or sometimes as *ghulams*, Arabic for "servant." Because Islam forbids the enslavement of Muslims, technically only non-Muslim boys were subject to such recruitment. After being enslaved, however, the youths were converted to Islam. They were then educated, trained, and raised to serve the dynasty. Such slaves could receive excellent educations and could and did rise to the highest ranks in the army and the palace. But since they were cut off from their families, clans, tribes, or other networks of support and owed their careers to the palace, these slave soldiers and servants generally posed little threat to the dynasts. Muslim dynasties from the Abbasids through the Ottomans with their famed Janissaries employed mamluk systems.

The Ottoman sultans may have been among the last to import slaves from the Caucasus, but they were not the first and were by no means alone. Dynasties throughout the Middle East relied on the Caucasus as a major source of slaves. The slave trade was one of the major links connecting and integrating the Caucasus with the wider world for centuries.[8] Hirotake Maeda provides in his contribution a rare close-up look at mamluks from the Caucasus in the nineteenth century. By this period multiple changes—technological, political, demographic, and normative—had been steadily undermining the mamluk system. In an age of mass armies and mass firepower slave soldiers no longer offered compelling military advantages. The system persisted, but its obsolescence had become clear.

Maeda offers us an inside look into how Caucasian mamluks in Egypt and Syria adapted to the changing conditions. To do this, he uses two case studies of mamluks. One is from a distinguished Armenian family from the Caucasus, the Enikolopians. The other is from Georgia, Ioseb Tsilosani. Mamluks, as Maeda informs us, were never wholly the possession of the ruling elite. Despite the conditions of their enslavement, upbringing, and service they retained ties of family, memory, and identity with their homelands. Mamluks remained, in practice if not in theory, intermediaries. When viewed through the set of understandings that frame the nation-state, the Enikolopians' career trajectories confuse and even disorient. The Enikolopians played prominent roles as elites in Georgian, Russian, and Qajar Persian societies. They crossed imperial state boundaries with seeming ease, receiving education in one empire before moving to take up administrative and diplomatic posts in another. Whereas state borders trump family ties in today's world, Maeda's investigation of the Enikolopians reveals a world of porous imperial state borders and enduring family connections.

Similarly, Maeda reveals that Georgian mamluks in Egypt often preserved connections with their homeland. Some were known to return to their birth country after achieving freedom, and still others maintained links with their siblings even while still in Egypt. The Georgian Ioseb Tsilosani was sold into slavery at age eight and given the name Ali Amedi upon his conversion to Islam. He was taught Ottoman Turkish and Arabic along with the Quranic sciences and later was sent to Europe to learn Italian and French. He never forgot his family, however, and while in Paris decided to pledge allegiance to the Tsar and return to Georgia. There, serving nominally as a Russian officer he put his linguistic skills to work as a translator. Tsilosani, like the Enikolopians, belonged to a complex set of overlapping constellations. His life cannot be reduced to that of a son of Georgia, slave of the Sultan, or officer of the Imperial Russian Army.

Given the prominence of the Caucasus as a source of slaves and as a conduit for their trafficking, it is perhaps an irony that the mountains and their inhabitants would in the modern world emerge as symbols of freedom. The image of the "freedom loving"—or "lawless"—mountaineer fired the imaginations of generations of young Russian men, among them some of Russia's greatest authors such as Lermontov, Pushkin, and Tolstoy.[9] As a land physically distant from the tsar's court and topographically distinct from the Russian steppe, the Caucasus came to represent an alternative world for Russia's disaffected nobility who served there as army officers. Russian writers began to portray the region's rebellious inhabitants, who were so exotically different from the Russians in their languages, dress, religion, customs, and social mores, as symbols through which they could express the Russian longing for freedom and anxieties about civilization and order. On the one hand, the Russians' struggle to subdue the stateless peoples of the Caucasus, particularly the Muslims, and integrate them into their empire assuaged anxieties about Russia's own level of civilization and development. If they could conquer foreign lands and build an empire from them in the same ways that the British, French, and other Europeans had done, it confirmed that they, too, were Europeans and representatives of an advanced civilization. On the other hand, the seeming freedom that the Caucasian peoples enjoyed by virtue of their living outside of autocracy and empire only highlighted the Russians' own servitude under the autocracy. Was the Russian advance into the Caucasus the advance of civilization against barbarism and lawlessness? Or was it the advance of despotism against freedom?

The Caucasus and Imperial Russia: A Transformative Encounter

By the sixteenth century, Russia had emerged as an actor in the commercial and diplomatic affairs of the Caucasus. Its influence in the region thereafter grew inexorably, albeit unevenly. It was in the nineteenth century that the projection of Russian Imperial power transformed the Caucasus and its peoples in a thoroughly far-reaching fashion. In 1801, St. Petersburg absorbed the Georgian territory of Kartli-Kakheti into the its empire. Shortly thereafter, it added the lands that make up contemporary Azerbaijan and Armenia. Thus, before the middle of the century Russia brought the whole of the Caucasus under unified and centralized rule for the first time.

Imperial Russia's encounter with the Caucasus profoundly changed Russia as well. In the words of Sean Pollock in the first essay, "despite its location at the edge of Russia's empire, the Caucasus was hardly peripheral to its concerns." The Caucasus, as mentioned above, loomed in the Russian imagination as a wild land filled with uncivilized, yet free and even noble people. As a topos it allowed Russian subjects to openly express and explore their misgivings and questions about the lack of freedom in their own society and the stifling effect of the Tsarist autocracy and bureaucracy even upon those whom it favored. The Caucasus impacted more than the literary and political imagination of Russians. In the sphere of official administration, the challenge of having to rule and administer the region—"a fissiparous frontier inhabited by ethnically and religiously diverse groups coveted by Russia and its imperial rivals in the region—that informed the policy of religious toleration" in Pollock's description—prodded the Tsarist regime to reduce its particularistic Eastern Orthodox Christian profile and adopt a more "universalistic" approach to governance. Pollock argues that Catherine the Great's famed "religious toleration," so often understood as the application of Enlightenment beliefs, also grew out of Russian officialdom's encounter in the eighteenth century with the reality of religious pluralism in the North Caucasus and its need to compete with imperial rivals in the region. Hence, St. Petersburg embraced a more secular framework in order to better accommodate its increasingly diverse populations. This policy of toleration did not disappear but was woven into the Russian practice of rule. Even as the Tsarist regime embarked on a war that would last more than three decades to crush North Caucasian mountaineers resisting its rule in the name of Islam, its efforts to defuse religious tensions facilitated its rule over Muslim populations elsewhere in the empire, such as in the South Caucasus and the Volga.[10]

Russian rule transformed far more than the borders and political landscape of the Caucasus. It altered profoundly the very physical landscape. Among other changes, in the North Caucasus the Russians built forts and later cities. They cut networks of roads through forests, and, as mentioned earlier, linked the North and South Caucasus more securely with the construction of the Georgian Military Highway from Vladikavkaz to Tiflis (Tbilisi). In the south, the arrival of the Imperial Russian bureaucracy in Tiflis at the beginning of the nineteenth century caused that provincial city to swell. Between 1876 and 1912 Tiflis increased nearly five-fold in population to just over three hundred thousand.[11]

There is no more vivid exhibit of the transformative impact of Imperial Russian rule than Baku. Prior to the arrival of Russians in 1806, Baku was a quiet coastal village. With a population under 5,000, it used to serve as a seasonal residence of the Shirvanshahs. By 1897, however, Baku had become a major industrial center. Its population numbered over 110,000, and it was producing as much as one half of the world's oil production. In 1913, the city's residents numbered nearly 215,000, and the value of goods passing through it surpassed that passing through any other Russian port, including St. Petersburg.[12]

It was not the exactly the "discovery" of oil that triggered Baku's explosive growth. The Apsheron Peninsula had been known in antiquity for its abundant surface oil pools and tar pits. Indeed, Zoroastrians had built temples where fires burned off gas escaping from the ground. Marco Polo among others reported stories of oil springs. The spark that ignited the oil boom was St. Petersburg's decision in 1872 to begin granting long-term oil concessions, thereby opening up the primitive oil industry there to private entities. The decision yielded immediate results. Entrepreneurs and investors flocked to Baku to make it rich with oil. In addition to Russian

Ossetian village

and local businessmen, Baku's oil industry attracted international investors such as the Nobel and the Rothschild families. The influx of capital and know-how fed explosive growth that made itself felt throughout the Caucasus and beyond. Baku's oil fields annually sucked in tens of thousands of laborers from throughout the Caucasus and Iran, converting peasants and shepherds into industrial workers and thereby introducing them to new ideas about social relationships, political organization, and legitimacy. Even as the industrialization of Baku generated the new constellation of proletariat, it also set in motion the reconfiguration of the constellation of South Caucasian Muslims. Drawn together in Baku from scattered villages and diverse landscapes and thrown together, Turkic-speaking Muslims found themselves a collective. To be sure, Islam had already defined them as a group, but in Baku they found not so much religious doctrine (about which many had only limited knowledge) mediated through religious experts binding them, or in the case of Sunni and Shi'a differences, dividing them, but rather the more direct and visceral links of a shared tongue and cultural practices. The genesis of a new constellation, the Azerbaijani nation, had begun.[13]

The need to transport Baku's oil to outside markets drove the development of industrial and administrative infrastructure throughout the rest of the South Caucasus. The famous Nobel brothers built the world's first successful oil tanker in 1878 to move oil more efficiently from Baku across the Caspian Sea to the port of Astrakhan on the Volga River. Tsarist authorities in the 1890s oversaw the construction of a railroad and pipeline linking Baku to the port of Batum on the Black Sea, from where Baku's oil could be shipped to world as well as Russian markets. Strategic concerns and the desire to safeguard Russia's burgeoning new investments prompted the construction of a railway from Tiflis to Kars to enable Russia's armies to traverse the Caucasus more rapidly. The new rail and port facilities in turn stimulated the exploitation and export of other natural resources, such as manganese, of which the region produced over one third of the world's total.[14] The construction and operation of railways and the opening of mines stoked further the demand for labor, managers, and capital.

The economic growth was intense and generated great wealth. Yet the oil fields and railroads of the South Caucasus represented in stark form the power of modern capitalism to enrich the few beyond their dreams and immiserate the many. The oil and railroad workers toiled under miserable conditions and were routinely subjected to exploitation.[15] Baku, perhaps inevitably, became a center of underground revolutionary activity and socialist agitation. The Bolsheviks, among others, used the city as a base from which to spread radical ideas of revolution throughout southern Russia and Iran.[16] One young Bolshevik Iosif Dzhugashvili, who later adopted the name "Stalin" meaning "man of steel" in Russian, distinguished himself as a loyal Bolshevik and effective leader while carrying out operations in Baku in 1907 and 1908.[17]

This socio-economic transformation had far-reaching political consequences. As Ronald Suny observes in chapter three, the very infrastructural, economic, and social developments that Russian Imperial rule had made possible were paradoxically undermining that rule in the South Caucasus already toward the end of the nineteenth century. The manifold changes drove the emergence of new class tensions and catalyzed ethno-national consciousness throughout the Caucasus. At the same time, the building of schools, the rise of literacy, the proliferation of printed materials, and the dissemination of new ideas of legitimacy, community, solidarity, and politics provided the peoples of the Caucasus with novel ways to conceptualize their own identities and those of their communities and to give voice to their aspirations and frustrations. As Suny notes in passing, an important arena for the transformation of Caucasian minds was outside the Caucasus, in the universities of Russia and sometimes Europe. Those universities introduced students from the Caucasus and elsewhere to unfamiliar, often radical, concepts of progress, nationhood, socialism, and revolution. Georgians who studied in Russia famously even came to be identified under a special name, the *tergdaleulni*, meaning "those who have tasted the Terek," or, in other words, those who have crossed the Terek River into Russia and beyond.[18] University education had no less a profound effect on Armenians, who came to play a substantial part in Russia's revolutionary underground. University-educated Armenians also began to reconfigure the constellation of the Armenian community, forging closer ties with Armenians in the Ottoman Empire and Persia and agitating for Armenian statehood in some form.[19]

Although this process of reconfiguration at the time of the Russian Revolution was significantly more advanced among the more literate Georgians and Armenians, it was nonetheless at work among the Muslims of the Caucasus as well. Graduates of Russian universities dominated the ranks of the founders of the Azerbaijan Democratic Republic and even of the leadership of the Union of the Allied Mountaineers of the North Caucasus. Here, again, whereas virtually all analyses of the Caucasus in the wake of the Russian Revolution organize their narratives around the category of ethnicity, along with an implicit *telos* pointing to ethno-national self-determination, it is important to recall that the majority of the political elites in the post-imperial polities were members another constellation, that of the Russian intelligentsia and of Russian Social Democracy.[20]

As the twentieth century dawned, those frustrations and aspirations were growing stronger and increasingly incompatible with the imperial autocracy. Belying notions of fixed communal identities extending back to the primeval past, a common trope in writings on the Caucasus and in the self-understandings of many of the region's inhabitants, Suny shows how the boundaries, definitions, and meanings of communal identities evolved. This is not an argument that socio-economic processes conjured the Georgian, Armenian, and Azerbaijani nations into being from nothing, but rather that the processes that Russian imperial rule made possible sharply altered the constellations of communal identity and thereby ushered in a new era in politics.

Islam and Authority in the North Caucasus: The Reconstitution of Constellations

The story of Russian imperial rule in the Caucasus is more than one of violence, disruption, and repression or of economic growth and infrastructural development. It is also a story of political, and even democratic, tutelage. In the Caucasus, as elsewhere in the empire, mass political parties emerged. Caucasians participated in the broader debates in imperial society about the future of the autocracy and the peoples who lived under it. The idea of dissolving the empire being difficult to entertain prior to World War I (and indeed even during the war), the leading Caucasian political figures saw their future as lying within Russia, albeit a democratic, not autocratic

Russia. Hence, despite the unraveling of the empire following the tsar's abdication in March 1917 and the subsequent *de facto* independence of the Caucasus, the inhabitants of the North and South Caucasus alike remained profoundly ambivalent about independence going into 1918.[21]

The Bolshevik seizure of power, however, spurred the peoples of the Caucasus to break formally from Russia in the spring of 1918. While the North Caucasians found their effort to establish a union of mountain peoples derailed by invasions from Bolshevik and anti-Bolshevik forces alike, the Azerbaijanis, Armenians, and Georgians managed to establish independent states in May and June of 1918. They did not last long, however. Small, fragile, embroiled in quarrels with each other, and having no possibility of outside support, they each succumbed to Bolshevik armies in less than three years. The Caucasus soon enough was again united and integrated into the Union of Soviet Socialist Republics.

The triumph of Bolshevism heralded a watershed in the region's history. The power that the Communist Party wielded through the Soviet state and the degree of control that it maintained over society were unprecedented. The Communist Party's ambitions for transforming society were likewise without earlier parallel in their aims and scope. Economic development and the acceleration of industrialization represented only the outward, physical manifestations of the revolutionaries' aims. The young Soviet cadres aimed to forge a wholly new society, indeed a wholly new human being.

For the Caucasus, two general policies pursued by the Soviet authorities were particularly significant: secularization and ethnicization. Militant secularization radically challenged, and changed, Muslim life in the North Caucasus. Although the interpretation and practice of Islam varied widely among the Muslim North Caucasians, Islam was inextricably interwoven, even if only in name, with their identities, both personal and communal, and with their rules of social conduct. The Communist Party, however, regarded all religions ultimately as pernicious anachronisms that would and should disappear. Soviet authorities banished religion from public life and heavily discouraged its practice even in private. Thus although the Bolsheviks initially permitted the Muslim religious authorities of the Caucasus significant latitude in the early 1920s, in 1926 Soviet authorities began a concerted campaign to suppress Islam throughout the Soviet Union including the Caucasus. They shuttered mosques, proscribed the veil, outlawed use of the Arabic script, and banned public rituals like the Shi'i commemoration of the martyrdom of Hussain. Communist agitators, such as the League of Militant Atheists, campaigned in public for the purging of Islam. Schools and workplaces became platforms for atheist propaganda. Teachers of Islam were sent to the Gulag, the network of Soviet penal camps established under Joseph Stalin.[22]

The ferocity of their policies notwithstanding, Soviet authorities never sought to strip Soviet Muslims of their religious identity entirely. Rather, they aimed to empty Muslim identity of any normative content and reduce it to one marker among others of ethno-national identity. On the progressive path to Socialism, all peoples, the Communist Party believed, were obliged to pass through a state of development characterized by the possession of a "national" consciousness. Thus, contrary to the simplified claim that the Soviets repressed national identities, it manifested an "ethnophilia," and insisted as a bureaucratic requirement that every Soviet subject adopt a nationality.[23] Thus in Dagestan alone, the authorities recognized fourteen distinct and official nations.[24] The promotion of ethnic identity had, from the Communist Party's perspective, the additional salutary effect of diminishing Islam's social and cultural influence.

Toward the ends of protecting the Socialist Revolution and its homeland, the Soviet state assiduously guarded its borders and curtailed communication with the outside world, particularly beginning in the 1930s. Whereas in the early years of their rule the Bolsheviks saw the Muslims of the Middle East and beyond as potential allies in the struggle against European imperialism, the contradictions between the materialist philosophy of Marxism-Leninism and the religion of Islam were too stark to ignore. Soviet authorities soon began to regard Islam outside the Soviet Union as an infectious source of counter-revolution, and so they took care to exercise their monopoly control over communication and information to effectively sever ties between their Muslim populations and those outside.

The consolidation of Soviet power and coerced isolation marked an unprecedented rupture in the history of Muslim Eurasia. The Caucasus and Central Asia from the earliest centuries of Islam had both figured prominently in the history of that civilization. The Central Asian cities of

Mosque at Yerevan

Bukhara, Samarkand and Tashkent won renown as centers of Islamic learning. The Caucasus, too, contributed substantively to Islamic civilization. The Dagestani city of Derbent had been part of the original caliphal empire in the seventh century and thus one of the oldest lands of Islam. Dagestan nurtured a high culture of Islamic and Arabic scholarship that was recognized even in Arabia. Right up until the formation of the Soviet Union, the Muslim populations of the Caucasus, Tatarstan, Central Asia, and elsewhere in Eurasia were still very much a part of the greater Muslim world.[25] Indeed, representatives from the Caucasus living in the Middle East were actively involved in movements ranging from socialist to Turkic nationalist and Muslim traditionalist to Salafi.[26] The rupture, thus, was culturally disorienting, and indeed among Moscow's motives in cutting contact with the outside world was precisely cultural disorientation. In the West, scholars tacitly assented to the new conceptual borders, as the study of the Caucasus and Central Asia was more often assigned to the broader field of Russian and Eastern European studies than to Middle Eastern or South Asian studies.

The fall of the Soviet Union permitted the Caucasus to reconstitute its ties with the broader Muslim world. The dissolution of Communist ideology, including its strictures against the belief in and practice of religion, preceded the dissolution of the Soviet Union. Thus, already in the 1980s a revival of public interest in Islam was evident.[27] The Soviet Union had never formally banned religious practice or study, but it did severely discourage the former and restrict the latter. One result was the creation of several generations of Soviet Muslims who identified as Muslims but were left poorly informed about the precepts and practice of their faith. With the lifting in the late 1980s of tight controls on borders and travel, Muslim Caucasians, predominantly young men, began travelling abroad to Arab and other Muslim countries to study and deepen their faith. Their return home provoked a crisis in religious authority. The severe decline in the quantity and quality of religious education in the Soviet period meant that the returning students, despite their youth, often possessed greater knowledge of the Quran and a superior command of Arabic.

The restoration of links with the broader Muslim world brought to the Caucasus many of the same debates, controversies, and struggles roiling Muslim communities around the globe. Prominent among these is the question of Salafi Islam, an austere school of Islam that in its interpretations favors literalism and assigns great importance to the examples set by the Prophet Muhammad, his companions, and the early generations of Muslims. Indeed, its name derives from the Arabic *salaf,* widely used to refer to the first three generations of Muslims. Salafism rejects as idolatrous innovations beliefs and practices introduced after these early generations. It has a wide following in the countries of the Arabian Peninsula, where it originated. Worldwide, it is perhaps the fastest growing school of Islam. It is therefore no surprise that Salafism has acquired adherents in Dagestan and elsewhere in the North Caucasus.

Although Salafism is sometimes described as a modern phenomenon, the fact is that many of its defining principles and tenets were formulated centuries earlier. Thus, for example, the thirteenth century theologian Ibn Taymiyyah was a formative figure in Salafi thought. Nor is Salafism wholly foreign to Dagestan. Dagestani religious scholars between the seventeenth and nineteenth centuries had been in direct contact and exchange with counterparts in Yemen who played key roles in the development of Salafi thought. The re-establishment of links with the broader Muslim world in the post-Soviet era, thus, has also reconstituted an old thread in the constellation of Caucasian Islam.

Salafism is an exacting form of Islam that presupposes a pristine Islam that must be rigorously cleansed of accretions. It sometimes carries with it a utopian flavor. Salafists are wary of compromise with forms of behavior and politics that do not fit their comparatively rigid standards. Consequently, Salafis often find themselves in opposition, passive or active, to local authorities. On a number of important theological questions, Salafism overlaps with Wahhabism, the school of Islam propagated in and by Saudi Arabia. Whereas the term Salafism, albeit not the doctrine, generally resonates positively among Muslims due to its root, *salaf,* Wahhabism does not. That name comes from Muhammad ibn abd al-Wahhab, a preacher from eighteenth century Arabia who advocated Salafi Islam.

As Michael Kemper and Shamil Shikhaliev discuss in their contribution, Dagestan's official religious establishment wields the label "Wahhabi" as a weapon to contain and suppress opponents and critics. In addition to carrying connotations of deviation from the proper or true Islam, the term Wahhabism also carries for Russia's Muslims connotations of foreignness and even hints of being an invention of Anglo-American imperialism. For over two decades as of this writing, the Republic of Dagestan has been plagued by persistent violence employed in the name of Islam. Studies of that violence are few, and among them there is a notable selection-bias in favor of attention to the rebel or opposition groups. Analyses of their opponents, the official state Islamic institutions and their Sufi supporters, are hard to come by. Kemper's and Shikhaliev's study of how the latter actors deploy the term "Wahhabi" to discredit and diminish their critics, including Muslims who abjure violence, is an exception. This research makes a major contribution to understanding religion and politics in Dagestan, as it is only through study of the varied parties and analysis of their interaction—as opposed to focusing solely on the armed opposition—that one can begin to understand what is a complex and multifaceted pattern of interaction. The dynamic at work in Dagestan of official religious authorities using peremptory accusations of "Wahhabism" or "fundamentalism" against dissident Muslims has parallels in a number of other societies. Kemper and Shikhaliev's study should therefore interest those working on intra-religious conflicts outside Dagestan and the Caucasus.

Indeed, in this context Dagestan is not exceptional. The greater Middle East at the time of writing is experiencing an era of horrific and now chronic sectarian strife and political breakdown, from North Africa through Syria to Pakistan and Afghanistan. As Kemper and Shikhaliev reveal, Dagestan and Dagestani Muslims are again part of a new and bigger constellation of religious conflicts, or, perhaps more accurately, conflicts with religious veneers. Not all constellations, alas, are felicitous.

Notes

1. This is not say that individual or even groups of Caucasians have never been at the center of empires.
2. John Colarusso, *Nart Sagas from the Caucasus* (Princeton: Princeton University Press, 2002), xiii–xv; 5–6; Geoffrey Lewis, ed. *The Book of Dede Korkut* (Harmondsworth, UK: Penguin, 1974), 9–23.
3. Bruce Grant, *The Captive and the Gift: Cultural Histories of Sovereignty in Russia and the Caucasus* (Ithaca, NY: Cornell University Press, 2009), 2–10.

4. Daniel G. Prior, "Travels of Mount Qāf: From Legend to 42° 0' N 79° 51' E," *Oriente Moderno* 89, no. 2 (2009): 425, 428, 430, 434.

5. Charles King, *The Ghost of Freedom: A History of the Caucasus* (New York: Oxford University Press, 2008), 136–39.

6. For attempts at general histories of the Caucasus, see King, *The Ghost of Freedom*; James Forsyth, *The Caucasus: A History* (Cambridge: Cambridge University Press, 2013). King's book dedicates the great bulk of its attention to the periods of Imperial Russian and Soviet rule. The encounter with Russia, and through Russia with European modernity, provides the general organizing focus. Forsyth's history aims to be more comprehensive and as a consequence is more sprawling.

7. "Constellation," *Merriam-Webster Dictionary*, accessed at http://www.merriam-webster.com/dictionary/constellation.

8. Liubov Kurtynova-D'Herlugnan, *The Tsar's Abolitionists: The Slave Trade in the Caucasus and Its Suppression* (Boston: Brill, 2010); Y. Hakan Erdem, *Slavery in the Ottoman Empire and Its Demise, 1800–1909* (Basingstoke: Macmillan, 1996).

9. Susan Layton, *Russian Empire and Literature: Conquest of the Caucasus from Pushkin to Tolstoy* (Cambridge: Cambridge University Press, 1995). See also Harsha Ram, *The Imperial Sublime: A Russian Poetics of Empire* (Madison, WI; Wisconsin University Press, 2006).

10. Michael A. Reynolds, "Muslim Mobilization in Imperial Russia's Caucasus," in *Islam and the European Empires*, ed. David Motadel, 187–212 (Cambridge: Cambridge University Press, 2014).

11. Dietrich Geyer, *Russian Imperialism: The Interaction of Domestic and Foreign Policy, 1860–1914*, trans. Bruce Little (New Haven: Yale University Press, 1987), 331.

12. Audrey Altstadt, "Baku: The Transformation of a Muslim Town," in *The City in Late Imperial Russia*, ed. Michael F. Hamm (Bloomington, IN: University of Indiana Press, 1986), 289. Geyer puts Baku's population in 1913 at 334,000. Geyer, *Russian Imperialism*, 331

13. Audrey L. Altstadt, *The Azerbaijani Turks: Power and Identity under Russian Rule* (Stanford, CA: Hoover Institution Press, 1992); Eva-Maria Auch, *Muslim-Untertan-Bürger: Identitätswandel in gesellschaftlichen Transformationsprozessen der muslimischen Ostprovinzen Südkaukasiens (Ende 18.-Anfang 20. Jh.)* (Wiesbaden: Reichert, 2004); Tadeusz Swietochowski, *Russian Azerbaijan, 1905–1920: The Shaping of National Identity in a Muslim Community* (Cambridge: Cambridge University Press, 1985).

14. Robert W. Tolf, *The Russian Rockefellers: The Saga of the Nobel Family and the Russian Oil Industry* (Stanford, CA: Hoover Institution Press, 1976), 118.

15. Sonya Mirzoyan and Candan Badem, *The Construction of the Tiflis-Aleksandropol-Kars Railway* (Leiden: Institute for Historical Justice and Reconciliation, 2013).

16. Moritz Deutschmann,. "Cultures of Statehood, Cultures of Revolution: Caucasian Revolutionaries in the Iranian Constitutional Movement, 1906–1911," *Ab Imperio* 2013, no. 2: 165–90; Cosroe Chaqueri, *The Russo-Caucasian Origins of the Iranian Left:*

Social Democracy in Modern Iran (Richmond: Curzon, 2001); Iago Gocheleishvili, "Georgian Sources on the Iranian Constitutional Revolution, 1905–1911: Sergo Gamdishvili's Memoirs of the Gilan Resistance," in *Iranian-Russian Encounters: Empires and Revolutions since 1800*, ed. Stephanie Cronin), 207–30 (New York: Routledge, 2013.

17. Ronald Suny, "A Journeyman for the Revolution: Stalin and the Labor Movement in Baku, June 1907–May 1908," *Soviet Studies* 23 no. 3 (1972): 394.

18. Suny explores the development of Georgian national sentiment and identity in detail in his book, *The Making of the Georgian Nation*, 2nd. ed. (Bloomington, IN: University of Indiana Press, [1988] 1994).

19. A useful overview of shifts in Armenian identity is Razmik Panossian, *From Kings and Priests to Merchants and Commissars* (London: Hurst and Co., 2006). Although now quite dated, Louise Nalbandian's classic study still remains useful: Louise Nalbandian, *The Armenian Revolutionary Movement: The Development of Armenian Political Parties through the Nineteenth Century* (Berkeley: University of California Press, 1963).

20. On the transformation of the North Caucasus under Russian rule, see Austin Jersild, *Orientalism and Empire: North Caucasus Peoples and the Georgian Frontier, 1845–1917* (Montreal: McGill Queen's University Press, 2002). More generally, see V. O. Bobrovnikov, *Musul'mane Severnogo Kavkaza: obychau pravo, nasilie* (Moskva: Vostochnaia literatura RAN, 2002).

21. Michael A. Reynolds, *Shattering Empires: The Clash and Collapse of the Ottoman and Russian Empires* (Cambridge: Cambridge University Press, 2011), 191–218; "Post-Imperial Politics, Islam, and Identity in the North Caucasus, 1917–1918," *Jahrbücher für Geschichte Osteuropas* 56:2 (2008): 221–47.

22. For a brief overview of the Soviet campaigns against Islam and the sometimes paradoxical role that Soviet scholarship played in them, see Vladimir Bobrovnikov, "The Contribution of Oriental Scholarship to the Soviet Anti-Islamic Discourse," in *The Heritage of Soviet Oriental Studies*, ed. Michael Kemper and Stephan Conemann, 66–85 (New York: Routledge, 2011); and Vladimir Bobrovnikov, Amir Nazruzov, and Shamil Shikhaliev, "Islamic Education in Soviet and Post-Soviet Dagestan," in *Islamic Education in the Soviet Union and Its Successor States*, ed. Michael Kemper, Raoul Motika, and Stefan Reichmuth, 107–67 (New York: Routledge, 2010), esp. 121–28. A concise overview of early Soviet policies on Islam in the South Caucasus is found in Rufat Sattarov, *Islam, State, and Society in Independent Azerbaijan* (Weisbaden: Recihert Verlag, 2009), 50–59.

23. On Soviet "ethnophilia" see Yuris Slezkine, "The USSR as a Communal Apartment, or How a Socialist State Promoted Ethnic Particularism," *Slavic Review* 53 no. 2 (Summer1994): 414–52. On Soviet nationalities policy more generally see Terry Martin, *The Affirmative Action Empire: Nations and Nationalism in the Soviet Union, 1923–1939* (Ithaca, NY: Cornell University Press, 2001).

24. Moshe Gammer, "From the Challenge of Nationalism to the Challenge of Islam: The Case of Daghestan," in *Ethno-Nationalism, Islam, and the State in the Caucasus: Post-Soviet Disorder*, ed. Moshe Gammer (London: Routledge, 2008), 179.

25. James Meyer, "Immigration, Return, and the Politics of Citizenship: Russian Muslims in the Ottoman Empire, 1870–1914." *International Journal of Middle East Studies* 39 (2007): 15–32. See also Meyer's *Turks Across Empires* (New York: Oxford University Press, 2014).

26. On the activities of the Kumyk socialist, future Bolshevik Dzhelal ed-Din Korkmasov in Istanbul, see Mehmet Perinçek and Arda Odabaşı, *Stambulskie Novosti'de Jön Türk Devrimi* (Istanbul: Kaykank Yayınları, 2013), esp. 23–66. On the Avar *'alim* and Naqshbandi sufi Nazhmuddin Gotsinskii's activities and ties in the Ottoman empire, see Donogo Xadzhi Murad, *Nazhmuddin Gotsinskii* (Makhachkala: DGPU, 2011), 71–93. Sonia Chesnin provides a brief but illuminating snapshot of intellectual culture of Dagestan in the late nineteenth century as a constellation of Islamic traditions from the Middle East in "Hasan al-Alqadari: The Last Representative of Traditional Learning in Daghestan," in *Daghestan and the World of Islam*, ed. Moshe Gammer and David J. Wasserstein (Helsinki: Academia Scientiarum Fennica, 2006), 81–94.

27. I write "public interest" because for long very little was known about how the beliefs and practices of Muslims in the Caucasus and other parts of the Soviet Union changed under Soviet rule. This is now changing. See this pioneering collection of eleven case studies of life in rural Muslim communities in the Soviet Union, Stéphane A. Dudoignon and Christian Noack, eds. *Allah's Kolkhozes: Migration, De-Stalinisation, Privatisation, and the New Muslim Congregations in the Soviet Realm (1950s-2000s)* (Berlin: Klaus Schwarz Verlag, 2014). On the Caucasus, see the essays in this volume by Vladimir Bobrovnikov, "Withering Heights: The Re-Islamization of a Kolkhoz Village in Dagestan," 367–97; and Shamil Shikhaliev, "Downward Mobilityand Spiritual Life: The Development of Sufism in the Context of Migration in the Context of Migration in Dagestan, 1940s–2000s," 398–420.

The Caucasus circa 1800

Friend and Foe: Religious Toleration in Northern Caucasia in the Age of Catherine the Great

SEAN POLLOCK

Historians trace the origins of a policy of religious toleration in the Russian Empire to the reign of Catherine II (1762–96). In framing discussion of the policy, they have tended to emphasize the Enlightenment, the power of ideas, and the role of the empress herself in bringing an end to state-sponsored religious persecution and in instituting a policy of religious toleration throughout the empire. Catherine has been depicted as a "student of the Enlightenment," an advocate of "the individual's right of religious liberty," and an "enlightened despot" who pursued "a program of religious toleration in the spirit of the 'well-ordered police state' imagined by the jurists of Central Europe."[1] In the case of Islam and its adherents, the empress has been credited with applying "'enlightened' principles of government to the pressing problem of Russia's Muslims," and with using "persuasion and political measures to gain their voluntary acceptance of Russian sovereignty."[2] Interestingly, having underscored Catherine's intellectual indebtedness to the Enlightenment, these same historians conclude that her approach to religious toleration was "ultimately pragmatic." Concerning Islam, Catherine's policy of religious toleration has been explained as "a response both to changing situations and to an increased appreciation and understanding of the problems and possibilities of [Russia's southern] frontier," an example of "accommodation" meant to "win over Muslim intermediaries who might assist the regime in securing this frontier and projecting power into the steppe."³ Similarly, Simon Dixon, who discusses the policy in a chapter titled "The Power of Ideas: Catherine and the *philosophes*," concludes that it was "not so much an Enlightened innovation as a belated recognition that religious suppression under Peter the Great and his daughter had been a counterproductive cause of civil unrest."⁴

Whether it was the power of ideas or the power of place—the challenge of a fissiparous frontier inhabited by ethnically and religiously diverse groups coveted by Russia and its imperial rivals in the region—that informed the policy of religious toleration, it is clear that Catherine's government implemented such a policy across much of Russia's expanding southern borderlands, from Crimea to the Kazakh steppe.⁵ But to what extent and how effectively did the tsarist state implement practices and policies of toleration in northern Caucasia, where it had established a presence as early as the sixteenth century? The present essay explores relations between the Russian government and the diverse peoples of Caucasia in the eighteenth century, and focuses on Russia's attempts to use religion as "an instrument of imperial rule."⁶ It draws on "revisionist" histories of early modern European religion, which emphasize the social and political factors that produced practices of religious toleration—understood not as a celebration of religious difference, but rather as acts of forbearance and even a kind of "charitable hatred"—in many places "before anybody managed to theorize about it."⁷ In doing so, the essay moves the discussion of Russian religious toleration away from the person and principles of Catherine II and toward the reality of religious pluralism and the exigencies of Russian imperial ambitions in Caucasia. In the first half of the essay, I argue that Russia's attempts to build its empire in the region required it to practice religious toleration prior to the formal articulation of the principles and institutionalization of religious toleration in Catherine's reign. Although Catherine's predecessors never issued a general statement of toleration of Islam nor followed a single policy toward all Muslims in northern Caucasia, they continued the Muscovite practice of using indigenous allies, regardless of confessional affiliation, to strengthen Russia's presence in the region. By the time Catherine came to power in 1762, Russian-Muslim coexistence and cooperation, no less than intermittent conflict, was a long-standing fact of life in northern Caucasia.

Lezgin

In the second half of the essay, I seek to show that Catherine's government inherited a strategy of co-opting Muslim powerbrokers and encouraging their conversion to Orthodoxy when possible as well as a set of local practices that tolerated Islam and allowed Muslims to play important, though circumscribed, roles as Russian empire-builders. The details of this strategy were worked out in the central administrative institutions in St. Petersburg, with the College of Foreign Affairs and the College of War playing the leading roles. In Caucasia, tsarist military officers, among whom Caucasian Muslims figured prominently, were responsible for implementing the strategy. In doing so, they had to balance the expectations of their superiors in the far-away capital with the need to meet the challenges generated by changing local circumstances that they could neither predict nor control. As a result, there was sometimes a gulf between what St. Petersburg hoped to achieve in the region and the order actually established. During her reign, Catherine's government extended Russian territorial claims in northern Caucasia and attempted to incorporate its people into the social fabric of the empire. By the end of the reign, however, neither a formal policy of toleration nor the government's attempts to instrumentalize Islam and use co-opted Muslim religious leaders to assimilate Caucasian Muslims to Russian institutions was sufficient to guarantee the peace and security of Russian subjects in the region. Instead, Russia's growing presence and imperial claims antagonized indigenous populations, whose leaders in response sometimes used Islam as a rallying cry against Russian encroachments.

Russian-Muslim Cooperation and the Conversion of Korgoka Konchokin

The Russian presence in northern Caucasia predated the reign of Catherine II and was predicated on a combination Russian military power—i.e., the threat of force—and cooperation between Russian officials and local notables, including Muslims. Aspiring to project power into a distant region of great ethnic and confessional diversity and possessing few servitors with experience in Caucasia, successive Russian governments pragmatically sought the cooperation of local elites regardless of confessional affiliation.

Prior to Catherine's reign, the modest Russian presence in northern Caucasia was concentrated in a single fort and several Cossack settlements located on the left bank of the lower course of the Terek River. The population of Fort Kizliar, established in 1735, reflected the diversity of the region. Among its founders was a Kabardian "prince," El'murza Bekovich-Cherkasskii (d. 1765). Unlike his more famous brother, Aleksandr Bekovich-Cherkasskii, a convert to Orthodoxy, El'murza remained "a fervent Muslim."[8] Having received his officer's sword in 1722 from the hand of Peter I, he rose to become a general in the imperial army and commander of the Terek-Kizliar Host. Five of his eldest sons served as army officers and as such were members of the imperial hereditary nobility; only one, K(h)asbulat, converted to Orthodoxy, possibly in order to marry the daughter of a converted Kabardian colonel in Russian service, a certain Andrei Ivanov (formerly Korgoka Konchokin, about whom more below).[9] Another son, Devlet-Girei, served as overlord among Chechens on the right bank of the Terek.[10] El'murza's nephew, Shelokh Kasimov, figured prominently among Russia's Muslim servitors, and it seems likely that a special study of El'murza's kinship and friendship circle would reveal the names of countless other such non-Russian, non-Christian servitors. Clearly, tsarist officials in northern Caucasia in the first half of the eighteenth century not only tolerated Islam, they sometimes professed it as well.

Kasimov's own story is instructive. The Russian government had maintained him as an *amanat*, or diplomatic hostage, at Sviatoi Krest in 1731, and later relocated him to Kizliar. Released to Kabarda in 1751, he soon petitioned the tsarist government to be taken into Russian suzerainty. In 1753 he was promoted to captain of the Kizliar Host. In addition to the salary he drew for military service, St. Petersburg granted him a "special salary," which consisted of 300 rubles per year, lumber and other building materials needed for the construction of a residence at Kizliar, and privileged access to forests, fisheries, and fertile lands in the vicinity of Kizliar. This was typical of the kinds of resources Russian authorities were prepared to commit to the maintenance of Kabardian notables in Russian service. It was hoped that Russian largesse would guarantee their loyalty and allegiance, provide incentive to them to serve zealously, and "entice other Kabardian chiefs to enter Her Imperial Majesty's eternal suzerainty and service" (*dlia priokhochivaniia protchikh kabardinskikh vladel'tsov k vyezdu v vechnoe e. i. v. poddanstvo i sluzhbu*).[11] Of course, the grants and other privileges provided by the Russian government to Caucasian notables depended on their perceived power and influence among their people. Kasimov's example would have highlighted to ambitious or desperate non-Russians the tangible benefits of Russian patronage. That Kasimov was Muslim appears to have been of little if any concern to Russian officials in the capital.

Exactly how Muslim the Russian presence in the region was prior to Catherine's reign is difficult to determine. Little is known about the life of Russia's Muslim subjects in Caucasia prior to the so-called "academic expeditions" of 1768–74. It is reasonable to conclude, however, that El'murza and his co-religionist fellow officers found ways of performing their religious obligations in and around Kizliar. In the 1770s, Kizliar was divided into eight quarters, at least half of which were inhabited by Muslims. In addition to Kizliar's Russian Orthodox places of worship, Georgian monastery, and Armenian church, there was at least one mosque; by the end of the century, there were more mosques (four) than Orthodox churches.[12] Thomas Barrett rightly emphasizes the appeal of such towns to non-Russians seeking trading privileges, protection from enemies, and permission to resettle closer to Russian positions.[13] There is every indication that toleration of non-Orthodox groups and confessional intermingling was a fact of life in Kizliar from its earliest days.

Kizliar also served as a refuge for escaped Christian captives and fugitive Muslims. Muslims willing to convert to Orthodoxy were welcomed to settle in the vicinity of Kizliar; those who refused to convert were returned on demand of their masters or else released "on bail" (*na poruki*) to Muslims residing in Kizliar "until the master's arrival." In 1763, for example, of the 33 fugitives identified as Muslims, only three converted to Orthodoxy, 22 were returned to their masters, and the remaining eight were entrusted to Muslim notables such as El'murza Bekovich-Cherkaskii and Shelokh Kasimov. Their subsequent fates are unknown, but it is likely they were put to work in the service of their guardians and Russian empire.[14] By 1768, it appears that the Russian government was allowing Muslim fugitives not willing to convert to Orthodoxy to settle in Kizliar on the condition that they pledge to reside there "eternally" and acknowledge Russian suzerainty.[15] Muslims would continue to seek and find refuge in Kizliar, to worship in its mosques, and contribute to—and sometimes thwart—efforts to build Russia's empire in the region throughout Catherine's reign.

While religious toleration was a prominent feature of Russian imperial practices in eighteenth-century northern Caucasia, tsarist officials did what they could to encourage the conversion of non-Russian Muslim notables to Orthodoxy. In the summer of 1759, a Kabardian notable named Korgoka Konchokin arrived at the Cossack *stanitsa* Schchedrin, located on the lower course of the Terek River. He was carrying a letter stating his desire to enter into negotiations with the commandant of Kizliar, Brigadier Ivan L'vovich von Frauendorf, concerning "an important matter." (Frauendorf had been serving at Kizliar since the early 1750s, and it is from his correspondence with the governor of Astrakhan and the College of Foreign Affairs that the fullest picture of subsequent events emerges.) While he waited out the mandatory quarantine imposed on highland notables wishing to enter Russian-held territory, Konchokin was visited by a number of Kabardians in Russian service. Since Konchokin could not speak or write Russian, these go-betweens—several Cossack officers and Konchokin's own sister—played vital roles in translating and conveying his intentions to tsarist officials. Shelokh Kasimov was among the first of these intermediaries to report back to Frauendorf. According to Kasimov, Konchokin had arrived at the border in order to declare his "sincere intention" to "accept the Russian Orthodox faith" (*priniat' grekorossisskii zakon*).[16]

Frauendorf was initially skeptical of Konchokin's stated intentions. He was concerned that Konchokin was simply looking for a pretext to travel to St. Petersburg in order to lodge complaints against his rivals in Greater Kabarda. The previous year, other notables from Little Kabarda, led by Batoka Tausultanov, had traveled to St. Petersburg to lodge a complaint against rivals in Greater Kabarda. In his petition to the Russian empress, Tausultanov had requested protection from these rivals and permission to resettle his people on the left bank of the Terek.

In principle, the College of Foreign Affairs was not opposed to the idea of resettling Kabardians on lands claimed by Russia. In a 1758 decree, the College stated that according to the 1739 Belgrade treaty with the Ottomans, "the Kabardian people were to be considered free," and that if "several Kabardian chiefs were ever to cross over to the Turkish side, it would not be possible for [the Russian government] to openly hinder this [movement]; likewise, the Turkish Court would have no just grounds for claims [against Russia], should any Kabardians wish to live on our side [of the Terek]."[17] The College was in favor of allowing Kabardians to resettle on Russian territory on the condition that they first accept the right of baptism into Orthodoxy. As the College explained in another decree, the Belgrade treaty prohibited both the Ottoman and the Russian governments from interfering in Kabardians' internal affairs. The Russian government had communicated this interpretation of the treaty to Kabardians through its representatives at Kizliar. In fact, Tausultanov had signaled to Frauendorf his readiness to "accept the Christian faith" as early as 1757, but refused to do so upon his arrival in St. Petersburg. Embroiled in the Seven Years War at the time, the College decided to put off consideration of the matter until "another more convenient time."[18] Clearly, the central government was looking for ways to encourage Kabardian immigration while claiming strict adherence to its treaties with the Ottomans. One way was to encourage Kabardians to become Christians.

Frauendorf, therefore, had no intention of allowing Konchokin to enter Russia until the latter's baptism into Orthodoxy was all but certain. Thus, Konchokin was subjected to another round of interrogations at the Shchedrin outpost, where he remained under quarantine. Other Kabardian go-betweens attested to the veracity of the story told to Kasimov. Following a medical examination and fumigation (*okurka*), Konchokin was permitted to travel to Kizliar, where he reiterated several times his readiness to be baptized. On 22 August 1759, under the supervision of Commandant Frauendorf and the clerical establishment at Kizliar, Konchokin was given the "Russian name" (*rossiiskoe imia*) Andrei Ivanov. (The inspiration for the surname apparently came from Frauendorf, who stood as godfather to Konchokin and whose own Christian name was Ivan.) From Frauendorf's perspective, and presumably that of his superiors in St. Petersburg, by accepting Orthodoxy, Konchokin was also acknowledging Russian suzerainty. Konchokin was now allowed to return to Kabarda to determine whether his wife and other kinsfolk would follow his example. He told Frauendorf that should his wife refuse to convert, he would send her back to her relatives. Konchokin was ordered to receive instruction in matters of faith while in Kabarda by the head of the Ossetian Commission, the Georgian cleric Pakhomii. In reporting the event to the governor of

Astrakhan, Frauendorf asked whether Konchokin should be sent on to St. Petersburg and requested guidance on enticing and rewarding those willing to follow Konchokin's example.[19]

In St. Petersburg, news of Konchokin's baptism was positively received at the highest levels of government. According to the head of the College of Foreign Affairs, Mikhail Vorontsov, Konchokin was "deserving of charity" since he was "the first Kabardian chief to be baptized." Still, Vorontsov and his colleagues reasoned that Konchokin, "being ignorant of Christianity," could not have agreed to be baptized out of religious conviction. Thus they instructed Frauendorf to investigate the "special reasons" that had caused Konchokin to take such an unusual step. Vorontsov also requested a full accounting of Konchokin's circumstances in Kabarda: "How many dependents does he have, and do his kinsmen wield power among the Kabardian people, and what are their fathers' names."[20] The Russian government was eager to cultivate clients in strategically important Kabarda but wanted at the same time to be able to claim faithful adherence to the terms of its treaties with the Ottoman government. Vorontsov reasoned that Konchokin's baptism had made it possible for St. Petersburg to do so. It is worth noting in this connection that the Russian correspondence concerning Konchokin is silent on the question of his confessional affiliation prior to arriving in Russia. Russian officials consistently avoided describing the process by which Konchokin came to profess Christianity as a "conversion," preferring instead the formula "accept the Russian faith and baptism" (*priniat' veru rossiiskago zakona i kreshchenie*). It is likely, however, that Konchokin, like his cousin, Islam (who Konchokin claimed also wished to be baptized), was in fact Muslim.[21] It is reasonable, therefore, to view his baptism into Orthodoxy also as a conversion from Islam. In Konchokin's case, Russian officials had good reason to avoid the term conversion, lest it appear Russia was engaged in proselytizing efforts among Kabardians, which might be interpreted by rivals as a violation of the terms of the Belgrade treaty. Russian imperial practice in the region was to tolerate Russia's Muslim subjects and to encourage non-Russian immigrants to convert.

The events surrounding Konchokin's conversion throw considerable light on the government's decision to strengthen Russia's Caucasian presence by establishing a new settlement at Mozdok, more than 100 miles upriver from Kizliar. The reasons behind the decision were outlined in opinions composed by the College of Foreign Affairs, forwarded to the Senate, and then summarized in a report confirmed by Catherine II on 9 October 1762 just a few months after the coup that brought her to power.[22] According to the College, the greatest challenge in the region was the reinforcement of Kizliar. Russian subjects needed to be protected against "local barbaric peoples" (*tamoshnikh varvarskikh narodov*). St. Petersburg had hoped the Ossetian Commission would be able to strengthen Russian security by persuading Caucasian highlanders to become Orthodox Christians, on the assumption that co-religionists would be more loyal to Russia than non-Christians would be. By 1762, however, the Commission's proselytizing efforts had borne little fruit. The Russian presence in the vicinity of Kizliar was relatively small and spread thin across several Cossack settlements located along the lower course of the Terek. At best these villages constituted a porous defensive line for Russia; at worst they served as targets for Caucasian raiders. Russia needed to increase the number of its (preferably Orthodox) subjects in order to fill in gaps in the border that was taking shape along the Terek.

The College viewed Konchokin's request to resettle his people at Mozdok as a "convenient means" of meeting this challenge. It hoped Konchokin's example would serve to attract other highlanders who, like him, were seeking to escape the oppression of local rivals and build securer lives for themselves under Russian protection. The new settlement at Mozdok would welcome "people of every nation, that is, Chechens, Kumyks and other highlanders and Nogai wishing to be baptized." Reconnaissance suggested that Konchokin and his cousins might bring as many as 800 people to Mozdok and that there were at least 3000 Ossetians and 1000 armed "Kist," or Ingush, horsemen who might follow their example. All these, it was hoped, would agree to accept both Russian Orthodoxy and Russian subjecthood. It was also hoped that Christian peoples, "Georgians, Armenians and others located beyond Russia's borders," would likewise wish to resettle on lands between Mozdok and the Cossack settlement at Chervlensk. Each nation (*natsiia*) would constitute a separate settlement (*sloboda*) and be permitted to build churches and worship according to its own faith. Muslims, however, would not be permitted to settle at Mozdok. But on this question the report undermined the goal of encouraging the

Christianization of Russia's Caucasian immigrants by providing salaries for Konchokin's retainers who refused to be baptized: those agreeing to be baptized were to receive 40 rubles, while those refusing to do so were to receive 30 rubles. In all likelihood, St. Petersburg intended to give local administrators latitude in implementing its policy, leaving enforcement of the anti-Muslim component of the plan to their discretion. As elsewhere in early modern Europe, Russian toleration meant supporting the dominant state religion—Orthodoxy—and making reluctant concessions in the case of other religions, including Islam.

There remained the question of how the Crimean and Ottoman governments would react to tsarist fort-building and settlement activities at Mozdok. The Senate anticipated this question by specifically referring to the "peace treaty concluded between the All-Russian Empire and the Ottoman Porte in 1739." The report faithfully summarized the contents of article 6 of the Belgrade treaty, which stipulated independence for Kabarda, that Kabarda serve as a "barrier" between the Russian and Ottoman empires, and that neither empire interfere in Kabarda's internal affairs. As for the lands around Mozdok, the Senate contended that they "incontestably belong to [Russia's] borders and are therefore convenient for settlement," a bold claim in light of the fact that the Russian presence in the region was modest, and that its "borders" there were a matter of imperial fiat. The Ottoman government would have no grounds for protesting the resettlement on Russian territory of a Kabardian chief who professed Christianity since article 8 of the Belgrade treaty, in Russia's view, sanctioned just such an event.

> If, after the conclusion and ratification of the present treaty of peace, subjects of either [signatory] Power should commit crimes or acts of insubordination or treason and flee to [the territory] of the other Empire, they shall in no way be received or protected but—excepting only those who may have become Christians in the Empire of the Russias and those who may have become Muslims in the Ottoman Empire—shall at once be returned or at least expelled from the lands where they may happen to be, so that such infamous men may produce neither coolness nor dispute between the two Empires.[23]

Chechen Women

The language of the article, however, raises questions about the Russian interpretation. The article does not specifically mention Kabardians, instead referring to fugitive "subjects of either empire." Since Kabardians were subject to neither empire, as stipulated elsewhere in the treaty, it would appear that article 8 does not apply to them. Alternatively, since Kabardians were independent, did that mean they could choose to become subjects of either power? Or did Russia's protection of Konchokin, given his acknowledged troubles with other Kabardians, constitute meddling in Kabarda's internal affairs in violation of the treaty? Though it was not immediately clear that either Crimea or the Porte would contest Konchokin's conversion or the new settlement at Mozdok, the Russian government deemed it prudent to prepare for such an outcome.

Aleksei Obreskov, Russia's resident minister in Istanbul, first learned of the events surrounding Konchokin's baptism and the founding of Mozdok from the vice-chancellor of the College of Foreign Affairs, Prince Aleksandr Golitsyn. In instructions to Obreskov, Golitsyn made frequent reference to the Belgrade treaty, indicating that Russia intended to live by its terms. He gave a brief account of recent events in northern Caucasia, explaining that chiefs in Little Kabarda had frequently petitioned Russia for protection from their rivals in Greater Kabarda. Next, he related the story of Batoka Tausultanov before moving on to outline the agreement reached with Konchokin. Golitsyn insisted that although Russia had never "openly" entered into Kabardian affairs, its officials had occasionally offered "advice" to Kabardian supplicants. The College was of the opinion that in most cases, Russian acquiescence to Kabardian requests to resettle within Russian domains would constitute a "violation of the current treaty with the Ottoman Porte." Konchokin, however, had been allowed to come to St. Petersburg and settle at Mozdok because he was the first Kabardian to accept Christianity "of his own will" (*samoproizvol'no*).[24] As far as the College was concerned, the Belgrade treaty sanctioned such acts.

The central government hoped Mozdok would serve as an observation post facing the Ottomans, much as Kizliar projected Russian power into the Iranian marchlands. Surrounded as it was by "many barbaric but brave nations," Kizliar required more people fit for military service, "especially Christians." The measures taken (mostly by Georgian proselytizers) to persuade Ossetians to become Christians, Golitsyn lamented, had mostly been in vain; those highlanders who had been baptized, in fact, continued to live "as pagans" (*v bezverii*). By settling Christian Kabardians at Mozdok, Russia hoped to provide both incentive and example to other highlanders. These newcomers would "not only come irrevocably under our suzerainty, but within the Christian fold in equal measure" (*a cherez to ne tolko priamo v nashem poddanstve bezvozvratno ostavatsia, no ravnomerno i v khristianskom zakone*).[25] It was with this in mind that Prince Andrei Cherkasskii-Konchokin had been allowed to settle at Mozdok approximately 65 miles upriver from the nearest Cossack outpost at Chervlensk.

As anticipated, Russia's rivals in the region viewed the matter differently. The Crimean khan complained to the Ottoman government that Russia was 1) keeping an army officer and Cossacks in Kabarda in violation of the Belgrade peace; 2) building a fortress on the Terek River; 3) subjugating the inhabitants of Little Kabarda by sending clerics to settle near Little Elbruz under the guise of hermits, when in fact their true mission was to promote Christianity in Greater Kabarda; 4) using violence to take Georgian captives from merchants passing through the region; and 5) supplying several border fortresses with troops, munitions, and provisions. In response to the complaint, the Porte demanded that Russia abandon its forts in the region and respect Kabardian independence.

Obreskov offered a point-by-point rebuttal of the complaint in a memorandum presented to the Ottoman government on 29 June 1764.[26] First, Russia was not violating the terms of the treaty by sending Cossacks from Astrakhan and Kizliar into Kabarda in order to take hostages and retrieve stolen property, but only exercising its right, as stipulated in the treaty, to continue this "ancient tradition."[27] Concerning the matter of Russia's fort-building activities on the Terek, Obreskov presented a drawing illustrating his government's view of the region's political geography (see Figure 1).

On the drawing, which plotted entire nations like flags on a map, Obreskov fixed Kabardian territory in the space located between lands inhabited by subjects of the Russian and Ottoman empires. According to Obreskov, Kabardian lands were bordered in the west by the Kuban River and in the east by the Kurpa River. The Russian government considered the peoples inhabiting lands to the west of Greater Kabarda to be Ottoman subjects (e.g., Circassians, Termirgoi, and Beslenei), and those to the east of Little Kabarda—"Kumyks, Chechens, and other Cossacks"—to be Russian subjects. Second, Russia was not building fortresses in the region but only "outposts," nor were these located anywhere near the confluence of the Terek and Kurpa rivers, but far downstream, near Cossack settlements. Such outposts were absolutely necessary, he explained, given the turbulent nature of Russia's Caucasian frontier, where Tatar nomads and highlanders were kidnapping Russian subjects, raiding Russian settlements, and robbing caravans passing through the region. These outposts served the essential function of protecting Russian lives and property. Mozdok was being built with these concerns in mind.[28]

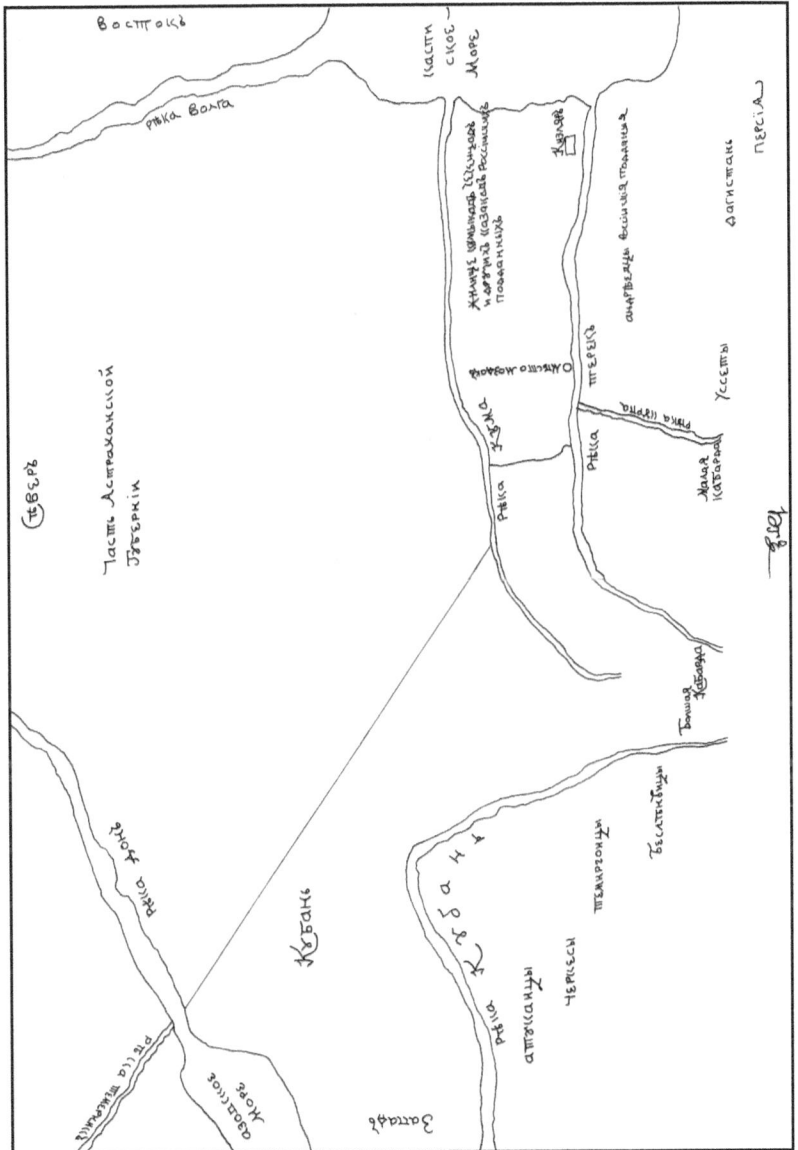

Figure 1. Aleksei Obreskov's Map of Northern Caucasia, 1764

As for Kabardians who had become Russian subjects, Obreskov argued, the treaty clearly recognized the right of individuals to choose their own religion and to settle in either empire—Christians in Russian lands, Muslims in Ottoman lands.[29] Finally, Obreskov addressed the issue of merchants traveling across the steppe between the Don River and Dagestan. He noted that Russia did not maintain forts south of the Terek, between Kabarda and Dagestan, so its officials could do nothing to impede travel in this region. Nor, he claimed, did his government have any knowledge of Georgian captives being taken into custody at Mozdok. On the other hand, Russia would not apologize for giving "refuge" to Christian slaves who managed to deliver themselves from Muslim captivity: "Muslims are prohibited from transporting Christian captives though Russian lands."[30] In subsequent reports to his handlers at the College, Obreskov emphasized the need to give more thought to defining Kabarda's borders and putting an end to the trans-Caucasian trade in Christian slaves. Should the government consider it politically expedient to allow this trade to continue, however, then Russia should in return demand the right to export its goods via the Dnepr River to Ochakov, and thence via the Black Sea through the Straits and into the Mediterranean Sea.[31] As these reports suggest, the interests of Christian slaves were not necessarily coterminous with those of the Russian state. In northern Caucasia, religion was important in so far as it could be used to advance Russian claims in the region.

Meanwhile, Prince Cherkasskii-Konchokin had arrived in Kizliar by April 1763. Within a few months, the official secretly charged with overseeing construction at Mozdok was reporting that the lords of Greater Kabarda had united to protest the project.[32] When their efforts to negotiate the termination of building operations at Mozdok failed, they threatened violence and sent a delegation to St. Petersburg for negotiations, which continued up to and during the First Russo-Turkish War of 1768–74.

Russian Military Colonization of Northern Caucasia and Attempts to Subjugate Kabarda

As far as the Russian government was concerned, the Russo-Turkish War of 1768–74 and the resulting peace treaty fundamentally changed the political status of Kabarda. Whereas the Belgrade treaty had proclaimed Kabardian independence, the Treaty of Küçük Kaynarca marked the end of that experiment. It fell to General Ivan de Medem, commander in chief of imperial forces in northern Caucasia, to convey the government's interpretation of the treaty to Kabarda's leaders. St. Petersburg informed Medem of its post-war policy in a secret rescript confirmed by Catherine on 5 September 1774. The government hoped the restoration of peace between Russia and the Porte would "naturally put a stop to the evil deeds of the barbaric peoples neighboring Kizliar and free you from the worry of having constantly to mobilize forces in defense of the lands under your guard." The government believed the key to peace in the region was to be found in certain articles of Russia's recent treaties and were eager for Caucasian highlanders, especially Kabardians and Kumyks, to learn the exact content and meaning of the treaties directly from Russian officials. The College therefore provided Medem with copies of the articles in Russian and "Tatar" "so that Kabardian chiefs would be able to read the exact words used in the treaties."[33] Article 3 of the Treaty of Küçük Kaynarca, Medem now learned, announced the independence of all Tatars in the Black Sea basin. The implied message for northern Caucasian peoples was that the Porte no longer had a political voice in the affairs of Crimea and the Kuban region. As for Kabarda — that great abstraction — it now belonged to Russia. This was how the government justified its claims in Kabarda:

> The treaty concluded with the Ottoman Porte, specifically article 21, says this about [the Kabardians]: 'Both Kabardas, that is, Greater and Little, on account of [their] proximity to the Tatars, have strong ties to the khans of Crimea; thus, their belonging to the Russian Imperial Court must be left to the will of the Crimean Khan, his Council and the elders of the Tatar nation.' The Crimean Khan, for his part, has already recognized the Kabardians' belonging to our scepter by the terms of the

treaty of friendship and alliance concluded with our plenipotentiary Lt. General Shcherbinin on 1 November 1772 (in [the negotiation of] which authorized Crimean and Nogai deputies, besides the khan, participated). Article 3 of the treaty with the Tatar region states exactly and precisely: 'All Tatar and Circassian peoples, Tamantsy and Nekrasovtsy, who, prior to the present war, were under the authority of the Crimean Khan, shall remain under the authority of the Crimean Khan as before; Greater and Little Kabarda, however, are under the suzerainty of the Russian Empire.'[34]

Anticipating the possibility, even likelihood, of divergent readings of the Küçük Kaynarca treaty, the College stated the policy with greater concision and clarity: "Kabardians, that is, the inhabitants of Greater and Little Kabarda, are to remain under our suzerainty." It worth noting that Kabardians were among the Caucasian peoples that Medem had subjugated in 1769 and 1770, an achievement proudly trumpeted in the newspapers of St. Petersburg.[35] Thus from the Russian perspective, the recent treaties did not so much cause a change in the status of Kabarda as provided legal justification for maintaining the status quo.

The College anticipated difficulties in getting Kabardians to accept Russian suzerainty, citing religious considerations as a complicating factor. It knew Kabardians to be fiercely independent and tied to Russia's Muslim rivals, Crimea and the Porte, "by a common religion, way of life, and to a certain degree, by nature itself." In contrast, their relationship with the Russian government had become almost entirely hostile. Mindful of this, the College instructed Medem to assure Kabardians that Russia would not seek retribution for past transgressions. Though deserving punishment, they would be spared "in the hope that by their future peaceful behavior they will answer for past deeds, and will remain loyal to us on the basis of the oath taken at the beginning of the recent war." St. Petersburg had no intention of interfering in Kabardians' internal affairs, wanting only to "count them among our subjects, in the same way their ancestors had voluntarily adhered to our empire from the earliest times." Russia was prepared to tolerate Kabardians and other "barbarians (*varvary*) and adherents of Islam" in the vicinity of Kizliar as long as they comported themselves peacefully. Finally, Medem was charged with leading the fight for Kabardian hearts and minds. He was instructed to treat Kabardians with "moderation, leniency, and fairness," so that they might accept Russian authority not only out of necessity but also as a result of reflecting on the benefits of doing so.[36] Among the benefits of Russian subjugation was freedom of worship, though this was not explicitly stated in the instructions to Medem. As we have seen, religious toleration was Russian policy in Caucasia prior to Catherine's reign. Her government understood that if it wanted to build Russia's empire in Caucasia, it could not afford to alienate the region's non-Christian peoples. On the contrary, it hoped that Islam and its adherents could be used to consolidate Russian power in the region.

Religious considerations, though, did not figure prominently in the initial plans to incorporate Caucasian lands and peoples into Russia. Following the war, Prince Grigorii A. Potemkin, as head of the War College and governor-general of Astrakhan, began to study the problem of Russia's border in northern Caucasia. In May 1776, he explained to Catherine that tsarist defenses near Mozdok were "extremely weak." According to his information they amounted to a mere 1640 Cossacks in thirteen settlements on the left bank of the Terek across a distance of more than 100 miles between Mozdok and Kizliar. Worse was the situation to the west. What Potemkin called the "border" (*granitsa*) stretching over 300 miles between Mozdok and Azov was "completely unprotected against Circassians and Kubantsy."[37] In other words, Potemkin was telling Catherine that Russia had no meaningful border in the Kuban steppe, only an open frontier. He therefore proposed to build a new fortified line across this space and to settle Cossacks from the Volga Host and retired soldiers on the lands behind it. These new arrivals, supplemented by regular troops already stationed in and around Astrakhan and Azov, would be enough, he argued, to guarantee the security of Russia's borders in the region.

Construction of the Line began in September 1777. As punishment for their part in the Pugachev Rebellion, the Volga Host was resettled from the Tsaritsyn Line (now abandoned) on lands located west of Mozdok and claimed by forces hostile to Russia. Their struggle for survival, Potemkin likely reasoned, would ultimately benefit the cause of Russian security. They laid the foundations for Forts Ekaterinsk (later renamed Ekaterinogradsk), Pavlovsk, Marinsk, Georgievsk, and Aleksandrovsk, all located

Circassian

between Mozdok and the Tomuzlovka River and completed by the end of 1777.[38] Each household was given a grant of 20 rubles to cover start-up expenses; by 1781 some 4,637 people resided in the new *stanitsa*s.[39] Further to the northwest, the Khoper Cossack Host was settled on lands between the Tomuzlovka and Egorlyk, where they built Forts Andreevsk (later renamed Severnaia) and Stavropolsk in 1778, and Forts Moskovsk and Donsk the following year. Fort Konstantinogorsk, on the Podkumok, was erected in 1780.[40] To improve defenses, palisades and earthen ramparts were built around the forts, and redoubts and observation posts were placed between the forts to facilitate communications. The settlement of these lands by Russian subjects was unprecedented in the history of the empire and marked the beginning of a new phase in the military colonization of northern Caucasia.

What impact would the new Line have on the region's indigenous groups? Those on the Russian side of the Line were expected to thrive, while those on the other side were to be weakened, cut off from their trading partners and traditional pasturelands. The stated purpose of the Line was to "protect against neighbors raiding the border between Astrakhan and the Don and the lands of our Kalmyks and Tatars, giving them the means to spread out all the way to the Black Forest and the Egorlyk [River] and thus access to better means of subsistence." In describing the Line, Potemkin acknowledged that it would "cut off various kinds of highland peoples"—specifically, Circassians, Abaza, and Kabardians, whom he depicted as "rapacious neighbors"—"from lands used for provisioning their livestock and herds," lands that "ought to be used by our subjects." Potemkin underscored the region's economic potential, which he presented as a farmers paradise, ideal for viticulture, the production of silk and paper, animal husbandry, horticulture, and arable farming. The Line would also make it easier to bring an end to the secret import of goods into Russia and facilitate the collection of taxes, thereby increasing state revenues. He also emphasized the strategic and military importance of the Line. It would protect Russia against invasion, facilitate the reinforcement of troops in Crimea and elsewhere, and open the road into the Caucasus Mountains, where some Ossetian notables were hoping to allow access to valuable mountain resources in exchange imperial protection. Finally, the Line promised to improve communications between the imperial center and the

Caucasian periphery by shortening the route from Mozdok to Moscow by over 300 miles and serving as a road to Azov.[41] Here was a plan to improve the Russian security and encourage economic prosperity in a region traditionally viewed by policymakers as a desert ringed by barbaric tribes. Interestingly, Potemkin said not a word about the religious profile of the region; the traditional practice of religious toleration would remain official policy there.

Not that freedom of worship was foremost in the minds of Kabardians and other indigenous groups confronted with Russian fort-building activities. In his reports of 1777, General Ivan Iakobi frequently claimed that Kabardians had not lodged any complaints about the construction work underway.[42] This left the impression that Kabardians were indifferent to the entire project. But Iakobi knew better. He was aware that in winter their herds required access to pasturelands lands located behind the Russian forts, that their livestock was their livelihood. "Should they be robbed of [their livestock], they would be robbed of all their property, for it consists in this alone."[43] In fact, during construction of the new Line, it was not uncommon for sizeable groups of armed horsemen (sometimes numbering in the thousands) to appear before the walls of the new forts. The first such sorties, carried out in the vicinity of the Malka River, bore little fruit. Undeterred, the Kabardian chiefs sought and found allies among the region's highlanders, including the Temirgoi and Beslenei tribes of western Circassia and Chechens and Kumyks to the east.[44] Their fortunes began to improve in the spring of 1779, when an army of highlanders crossed the Malka and set up camp on the Zolka River not far from Fort Marinsk. Their demand was straightforward: the demolition of Russian forts in the Terek-Kuban basin. They attempted to sever communications between Marinsk and Ekaterinsk, killing dozens of imperial troops and driving off several thousand head of livestock in the process. Further north, Andreevsk and Stavropolsk came under attack. At first Russian forces were hesitant to engage the enemy, as Potemkin had ordered Iakobi to assume a defensive posture at least until September.[45] Iakobi decided to await the arrival of reinforcements before mounting a robust defense.[46] Meanwhile, he authorized officials in Kizliar to imprison the town's Kabardian population and to place the adult diplomatic hostages in iron shackles, "so that they might feel their fathers' impertinence." This desperate step, however, did nothing to improve the situation in Kabarda. In June as many as 15,000 highlanders laid siege to Marinsk, forcing Iakobi to take action. On June 10, after six hours of fierce fighting, his forces managed to repulse the attackers. The battle had been a lopsided affair, with the highlanders suffering far greater losses. After a month of relative tranquility, the highlanders returned to the Line to demand an end to the Russian occupation of lands between Mozdok and Stavropolsk. They complained that the new forts had been built on lands where they pastured their herds in winter, when cold and snow forced them down from the mountains and onto the grassy steppe. Iakobi had neither the inclination nor the authority to satisfy their demands, so the cycle of violence continued into the fall.[47]

After a major battle with highlanders on the Malka River, Iakobi led his army of several thousand up the Baksan valley in order to capitalize on Kabardian losses. The conditions were far from ideal; heavy snow and a strong frost made for tough going. On 30 November the army reached the mountains where Kabardian forces were encamped. There Iakobi received a deputation from "princes" Misost and Shamgar, who were prepared to surrender. "When we arrived, they began to plead insistently [for mercy], promising to sign anything we liked and swear fealty. Negotiations concluded with the signing of a peace. All the princes swore fealty in the presence of the troops and signed, although reluctantly, an agreement that was not at all to their advantage."[48]

The "agreement" forced Kabardians to acknowledge Russian suzerainty and borders that, interestingly, distinguished between Kabarda, now part of the Russian Empire, and Russia proper. It also aimed to protect Caucasian supplicants willing to become Christians and to use Islam to guarantee Kabardian acceptance of Russian demands. The "peace" obliged Kabardians to return livestock, money, and captives taken by various highland groups over the past few years (articles 1–2).[49] Article 4 provided that the Malka River serve as the border between Kabarda and Russia and enjoined Kabardians from pasturing their herds or cultivating lands north of the river. Other articles attempted to restrict Kabardians' access to the Line and the lands beyond it; to oblige them, as "eternal subjects of Her Majesty," to execute all Imperial orders; and to circumscribe their relations with the Tatars of the Kuban and the Temirgoi and Beslenei of western Circassia (articles 5–8). Articles 9 and 10 granted to Kabardian peasants and

Ossetians the right to seek "refuge and protection" on the Line, should either persecution by their masters or a desire to be baptized into Orthodoxy motivate their flight from Kabarda. Finally, Kabardian leaders had recourse for wrongs committed against them to their elder chief Dzhankhot Tatarkhanov and the Imperial bailiff for Kabardian affairs, Dmitrii Taganov (article 11). Days later a similar agreement was reached with the chiefs of Little Kabarda. That agreement stipulated that the Terek serve as the border between Russia and their domains.[50] The leaders of both Kabardas swore to uphold the articles of the agreements, which defined them as Russian subjects, "before the Holy Koran, almighty God, and His Prophet Mohammed" (article 13). In this way, the Russian government sought to use Islam as a tool to effect the subjugation of the Kabardian people.

In the oath of fealty they were forced to sign, the people of Little Kabarda repented for having participated in the "revolt and mutiny" (*miatezh i bunt*) of the previous summer; stealing Imperial property; demanding the destruction of Russia's forts; and refusing to acknowledge their status as Russian subjects. Further, they acknowledged that future transgressions would have the gravest consequences. "Should we violate in any way this sworn oath, then we renounce forever almighty God and our Prophet Mohammed, and as unbelievers, lose for now and forever the favor of almighty God and the Great Prophet Mohammed, and subject ourselves to eternal damnation, as well as to the punishment of the invincible arms of Her Imperial Majesty."[51] To betray their sworn oath to Russia was to betray their God; in other words, to renounce their ties to the Russian Empire was to renounce their ties to Islam.

Islam and Creation of Clan Courts in Kabarda

Following the death of Prince Potemkin in 1791, the Russian government increased efforts to incorporate Kabarda into the Russian Empire, using Islam and Muslims in Russian service to achieve that end. The details were worked out by the College of Foreign Affairs and General Ivan Vasil'evich Gudovich, who was given the Caucasia portfolio. Russia at the time was fighting another war with the Ottomans, and the security situation in northern Caucasia greatly troubled the general and his handlers in St. Petersburg.

The problem was especially acute along the lower course of the Kuban River: two hundred miles separated the westernmost Russian fort, Grigoripolis, from the mouth of the river; between these points there was "not a single abode." Russian officials were aware that native groups periodically forded the river en route to the salt lakes and pastures located north of its right bank, but were unable to detect any patterns in their practice of pastoral transhumance. Gudovich, for example, saw only "disorderliness, frivolity, and anarchy" in the natives' way of life. In order to secure Russia's borders, the College instructed him to settle a Cossack regiment on the Kuban River, as had previously been done in the Terek basin, and suggested moving Tatar groups from the Kuban steppe to Molochnye Vody, in Tauris district. The College left it to Gudovich to propose where to build the new forts and how many troops to keep in the region. "As for Russia's subject borderland peoples (*poddannykh Rossii pogranichnykh narodov*), governors-general may gradually introduce institutions and courts, as has been done in the case of the Kirghiz (i.e., Kazakh) people, but only in accordance with the expressed desire and free will of those peoples."[52] With these guidelines in mind, Gudovich began to study Russia's defenses in the Terek-Kuban basin and its relations with neighboring peoples.

In January 1792, he drafted a proposal aimed at strengthening Russia's Caucasian frontier and establishing Imperial order in Kabarda. The first challenge, according to Gudovich, was to secure communications between the Kuban and Don Rivers (he noted that highlanders were often encountered on the road leading to Cherkask) and to protect Russian settlements along the Terek. He aimed to improve security on the Line by strengthening its fortresses and increasing its population. He proposed to settle 3,000 Don Cossacks on the Kuban (these would later be known as the Kuban or Black Sea Cossack Host) and expand several fortresses there. Having thereby secured the Line, the next step would be to settle state peasants and build churches on the lands behind it. It did not occur to Gudovich that these new settlements, whose purpose was to strengthen Russia's defenses against neighbors' raids, might serve instead to encourage them. But in this he was no different than his predecessors.[53]

The problem with Kabarda, as framed by Gudovich, was the way of life of its people. Their customs were "depraved" (*razvratnye*), their way of life, "disorderly" (*bezporiadochnyi*). Unlike Russia, Kabarda had neither a central government nor courts to regulate its affairs. "From their earliest childhood they are raised to think only of acquiring a bow, rifle, saber and a coat of mail, all for killing each other and [their] neighbors," Gudovich imagined. This made them "harmful to themselves and to those who have settled on the Line." In order to bring an end to this anarchy, the general recommended establishing clan-based courts, to be run by Kabardian chiefs, their retainers, and two Russian officers. Disputes of relatively minor significance would be decided according to their own customs. Major offenses, including treason, murder, and brigandage, would be prosecuted under Imperial laws. Besides their obvious purpose as a means to establish Russian law and order in Kabarda, these courts had a civilizing mission to perform as well: namely, to "prompt [Kabardians] to engage in industry, farming, and animal husbandry." Finally, under Gudovich's system, Kabardians would be prohibited from convening assemblies of the land and bearing arms on Russian territory or near its borders.[54]

Catherine approved the proposal in a February 1792 decree addressed to Gudovich as the newly appointed governor-general of Caucasia (he continued to serve as governor-general of Tambov and Riazan as well). In the decree, Catherine acknowledged persistent problems in Kabarda. Like Gudovich, she traced the source of the problems to Kabarda's "intrinsic anarchy," which for her explained why "up to now this people could not be put to good use," and why Kabardians had been a constant thorn in Russia's side. She recognized that arms alone could not defeat "peoples living in inaccessible mountains and having in them safe refuge from our troops." In such cases, she found it convenient to have recourse to ideological weapons: notions such as "philanthropy" (*chelovekoliubie*), "law" (*pravosudie*), "justice" (*spravedlivost'*), and "meekness" (*krotost'*).[55] But how was Gudovich to put these principles into practice? Catherine instructed the governor-general to adopt the following approach:

1) To cajole and attract to us in every way possible the best people of this nation; those who demonstrate more loyalty to us shall be allowed to make representations [to the government] and consequently shall be granted ranks, money and other marks of distinction as deemed expedient. Still more royal favors shall be bestowed on those who voluntarily adopt the

Christian faith. 2) To insure that neither our troops nor the Cossacks who are on the Line give any offense or cause any hardship to the highlanders arriving at our fortresses.... 3) To establish courts (*sudy*) among them according to the number of clans: for the chieftains, under the name "Kabardian court of the so-and-so clan;" and for the retainers, "clan courts" (*rodovye raspravy*), to be composed of their best people, as chosen by themselves, attaching none of our officers to them, following the example of the courts that have been established to advantage in Orenburg among the Kirgiz, and to promise them a salary as well.

From this it is clear that Catherine's government was prepared to tolerate non-Orthodox faiths in Kabarda and at the same time sought to give Kabardians incentives to convert to Orthodoxy. To achieve her government's ends, Catherine recommended establishing a "Supreme Border Court" in either Mozdok or Ekaterinograd. The best way to "win [Kabardians'] hearts," she instructed, was by reasoned "persuasion" rather than physical coercion. She hoped that Gudovich would be able to convince Kabardians of the merits of the proposed reforms so that they themselves would formally request implementation.[56]

In St. Petersburg to coordinate policy with the central government, Gudovich proposed setting up two courts for the chiefs and two courts for the retainers in Greater Kabarda, and one for each of these groups in Little Kabarda. Kabardians themselves would be responsible for operating the courts. The purpose of the courts was to establish "order and subordination among [Kabardians]." The "order" Gudovich had in mind was a mix of Kabardian customary law and Russian law; in other words, he aimed to subordinate them to authority in general, both Kabardian and Russian. In his proposal, Gudovich was careful to note that "all the clans of the chiefs and retainers of Greater and Little Kabarda requested by letters sent to me of their own free will the establishment of clan courts among them." This meant that Catherine's government could claim that it was building its empire in Kabarda by invitation rather than force. In addition to the clan courts, Gudovich proposed setting up a Supreme Border Court in Mozdok with the fort's commandant serving as chair. Besides Kabardians, Georgians, Armenians, and Tatars would also have representatives on this court. These proposals were approved by imperial decree on 19 April 1793.[57]

Back in Caucasia, Gudovich supervised fortification work and prepared Kabardians to receive the new legal institutions they had ostensibly requested. In opening the courts, Gudovich had had to spend considerable time explaining their purpose and mechanics to the people of Kabarda.[58] In this the mufti of Orenburg, Mukhamedzhan Khusainov (1756–1824), played an important role; in April of the following year he was presented with a medal for this work and given leave to return to his see.[59] Gudovich's administration initially appeared to be making progress in strengthening Russia's Caucasian borders and integrating Kabarda into the legal framework of the Empire. Gudovich proposed building an additional twelve forts and redoubts on the Line, but St. Petersburg called a halt to further major fortification work, believing that Russia already possessed a "sufficient barrier" in the region.[60] It seems Catherine's government was now satisfied to have the Kuban, Malka, and Terek Rivers serve as Russia's borders in region.

Not everyone in Kabarda cheered the new order embodied in the clan courts, however. "Karabrdians are inclining toward rebellion," Gudovich reported just a few months after opening the courts. He blamed an Ottoman *firman* and a letter from Murad Giray Sultan, "who calls himself the Porte's commander of all the Transkuban peoples," for fomenting rebellion in Kabarda.[61] By the summer of 1794, more than a thousand Kabardians were meeting in "forbidden assemblies" and committing "treason" by agreeing among themselves to ignore the new courts in favor of establishing one religious court. The situation in Greater Kabarda was especially chaotic.[62] Among the leaders of the resistance were two of the highest ranking Kabardians in Russian service: Lt. Colonel Atazhuko Khamurzin (who had distinguished himself in battle near the Danube in 1791) and Premier Major Adil Giray Atazhukin, the leaders of the Zhanbulat and Atazhukin clans, respectively. Both had recently been elected to serve as judges on the clan courts, and both, presumably, were Muslim.[63] Gudovich reacted by arresting the leaders he could find and stripping them of their ranks as well as their status as chiefs of among their own people, appointing others in their place.

These measures failed to bring an end to the rebellion, however. Kabardians continued to demand the removal of the clan courts.⁶⁴ Unfortunately for Gudovich, Kabardian resistance to Russian reforms coincided with the rise of Aga Mohammad Khan in Iran. By 1795, it was becoming increasingly difficult to ignore the threat he posed to Russian interests in southern Caucasia. Gudovich's reports from the field in the years 1795 and 1796 suggest that the more he became involved in monitoring the situation in Iran, the less he was able to follow through on his plans in Kabarda. By the time he quit the region, soon after September 1796, the prospect of establishing imperial order in Kabarda looked dim.

Conclusion

As the Russian government became increasingly involved in northern Caucasia in the eighteenth century, it was forced to confront the region's great ethnic and confessional diversity. In particular, this meant coming to terms with Islam, the predominant monotheistic faith of the region's elites. Complicating matters for Russia was the fact that these elites had historical and cultural ties to Russia's Muslim rivals for power in Caucasia: the Crimea Khanate, the Ottoman Empire, and Persia. Given the distance—physical, cultural, and otherwise—that separated the Russian center from Caucasia, as well as the limited resources at the state's disposal, it was imperative that Russian policy and practice take these factors into consideration. If Russia was to build its empire in northern Caucasia, it needed to win Muslim (and other non-Orthodox) friends and manage Muslim foes. Religious toleration was one means to this end.

In the present essay I have attempted to show that long before Catherine II came to power, religious toleration was enshrined in Russian imperial practices in northern Caucasia. Although more research is needed to determine the extent of Russian-Muslim cooperation in the region in the first half of the eighteenth century, it is clear that Muslim notables such as El'-murza Bekovich-Cherkasskii and Shelokh Kasimov played important roles in building Russia's empire there, and that Kizliar was home to a sizeable Muslim community and served to attract Muslim and Christian refugees alike. Even as the Russian government sought to convert Muslims, as in the case of Korgoka Konchokin, it made allowance for those who were

Vladikavkaz, at the foot of the Caucasus

willing to serve Russian interests but unwilling to convert to Orthodoxy. Under Catherine, the Russian government claimed suzerainty over Kabarda and pledged to tolerate (*terpet'*) Kabardians' adherence to Islam. Indeed, as the 1779 "agreements" reached between Russia and Kabardians demonstrate, Catherine's government saw utility in Islam, a means to bind Muslims to the Russian body politic. The instrumentalization of Islam by Catherine's government found fullest expression in attempts to create clan courts in Kabarda. Despite the efforts of the mufti of Orenburg to lend Islamic legitimacy to the project, however, Kabardians, led by Muslim officers in Russian service, ultimately rejected the Russian-sponsored courts, thereby revealing the limits of religious toleration as a means of assimilating Caucasian Muslims into the Russian Empire.

Clearly, expediency, rather than philosophical commitment, informed the practice of Russian religious toleration in northern Caucasia in the eighteenth century. The same may be said of Catherine II's famous pronouncements on religious toleration. In 1767 she instructed the Legislative Commission on the virtue of a "wise Toleration" in an empire as vast and diverse as Russia. For Catherine religious toleration was not an end in itself, but a means of achieving "the Peace and Security of [Russia's] Subjects."[65] Several years later, in 1773, the Holy Synod issued a decree declaring toleration for "all confessions." The decree was issued in response to a dispute that had arisen between civil and ecclesiastical authorities in Kazan. The governor of the region, citing the articles of Catherine's *Instruction* quoted above, had given permission to build two mosques, thereby distressing Orthodox officials in the city. The Synod confirmed the governor's decision and prohibited Orthodox officials from interfering in questions pertaining to non-Orthodox confessions and houses of worship, which were under the jurisdiction of civil administrations.[66] The decree, then, was one in a series of ad hoc decisions made in response to changing circumstances, a consequence of the need to manage Russia's confessional diversity. In such decrees, as Isabel de Madariaga has observed in the context of *Instruction*, "Catherine expressed strictly utilitarian as distinct from theological maxims."[67] For Catherine, who according to Madariaga "was probably an agnostic" and on whom "religion sat lightly," religious questions impacting the lives of Russian subjects were essentially political. And for Catherine, according to her secretary Aleksandr Vasil'evich Khrapovitskii, "all politics is founded on three words: circumstance, conjecture, and conjuncture."[68] In promoting religious toleration in Russia, Catherine was more a Machiavellian prince than she was an Enlightened *philosophe*.

Parallels can be drawn between tolerationist practices in early modern Europe and Russia. As Mary Fullbrook has suggested, "the problem of religious toleration cannot be treated purely as a question in the history of ideas.... Policies of religious uniformity or toleration depend to a considerable extent on the historically contingent constellations of relationships among state, church, and social groups as they developed in different areas in post-Reformation Europe."[69] In general, historians of early modern Europe tend to treat religious toleration not as an ideological or philosophical commitment, but "a social practice, a pattern of interaction among people of different faiths."[70] Similarly, in Russia, the present essay has shown that tolerationist practices emerged in northern Caucasia as a result of interactions among the state, the church, and an array of local social groups. In Russia's attempt to build its empire in often restive northern Caucasia, religious toleration was a means of ordering relations among people of different faiths. As in Europe, toleration in Russia was "a pragmatic move, a grudging acceptance of unpleasant realities, not a positive virtue."[71] For Russia, the "unpleasant reality" in northern Caucasia was the predominance of Islam among its most powerful groups and Russia's imperial rivals for power in the region. In Russia, toleration of Islam was not a virtue, nor did it proceed from indifference or neutrality. As the passages quoted from Catherine's *Instruction* suggest, to tolerate was "to permit or license something of which one emphatically disapproved, to make a magnanimous concession to the adherents of an inherently false religion."[72] The challenge that non-Orthodox faiths posed to Russian empire-building, however, was not insurmountable. As in Europe, there was space in Russia for discourses of qualified toleration and forbearance.[73] And is in Europe, where "ideas and practices of tolerance and toleration were available and in use long before the Enlightenment" and were "dialectically and symbolically linked" to those of intolerance,[74] tolerationist ideas and practices were available and in use in Russia before Catherine II came to power and coexisted with those of intolerance. In northern Caucasia, Russian toleration predated the advent of Catherine II and dovetailed nicely with her commitment to rational policymaking and qualified religious accommodation.

Notes

1. Gregory L. Bruess, "Religious Toleration in the Reign of Catherine the Great," in *International Perspectives on Church and State*, ed. Menachem Mor (Studies in Jewish Civilizaton—4; Omaha: Center for the Study of Religion and Society, Creighton University Press; New York: Fordham University Press, 1993), 299; and Robert D. Crews, *For Prophet and Tsar: Islam and Empire in Russia and Central Asia* (Cambridge: Harvard University Press, 2006), 32–33.
2. Alan W. Fisher, "Enlightened Despotism and Islam under Catherine II," *Slavic Review* 27, no. 4 (1968): 542.
3. Bruess, "Religious Toleration," 299; Fisher, "Enlightened Despotism," 552; Crews, *For Prophet and Tsar*, 33.
4. Simon Dixon, *Catherine the Great* (Harlow, England: Longman, 2001), 79. A similar conclusion is reached in Andreas Kappeler, "Czarist Policy toward the Muslims of the Russian Empire," in *Muslim Communities Reemerge: Historical Perspectives on Nationality, Politics, and Opposition in the Former Soviet Union and Yugoslavia*, ed. Andreas Kappeler, Gerhard Simon, Georg Brunner and Edward Allworth, (Durham: Duke University Press, 1994), 146; Michael Khodarkovsky, "The Conversion of Non-Christians in Early Modern Russia," in *Of Religion and Empire: Missions, Conversion, and Tolerance in Tsarist Russia*, ed. Robert P. Geraci and Michael Khodarkovsky (Ithaca: Cornell University Press, 2001), 138; and Vladimir Bobrovnikov, "Islam in the Russian Empire," in *The Cambridge History of Russia*, vol. II, *Imperial Russia, 1689–1917*, ed. Dominic Lieven (Cambridge: Cambridge University Press, 2006), 207. On the influence of the European Enlightenment on Russian thought, see G. M. Hamburg, "Religious Toleration in Russian Thought 1520–1825," *Kritika: Explorations in Russian and Eurasian History* 13, no. 3 (Summer 2012): 515–59.
5. See, for example, Fisher, "Enlightened Despotism;" Crews, *For Prophet and Tsar*, ch. 1; Charles Steinwedel, "How Bashkiria Became Part of European Russia, 1762–1881," in *Russian Empire: Space, People, Power, 1700–1930*, ed. Jane Burbank, Mark von Hagen, and Anatoly Remnev (Bloomington: Indiana University Press, 2007), 98–101.
6. I borrow the phrase from Crews, *For Prophet and Tsar*, 2.
7. See for example Ole Peter Grell, Jonathan I. Israel, and Nicholas Tyacke, eds., *From Persecution to Toleration: The Glorious Revolution and Religion in England* (New York: Oxford University Press, 1991); Ole Peter Grell and Bob Scribner, eds., *Tolerance and Intolerance in the European Reformation* (New York: Cambridge University Press, 1996); Ole Peter Grell and Roy Porter, eds., *Toleration in Enlightenment Europe* (New York: Cambridge University Press, 2000); John Coffey, *Persecution and Toleration in Protestant England, 1558–1689* (New York: Longman, 2000); and Alexandra Walsham, *Charitable Hatred: Tolerance and Intolerance in England, 1500–1700* (Manchester: Manchester University Press, 2006). The final quotation is from John Christian Laursen and Cary J. Nederman, eds., *Beyond the Persecuting Society: Religious Toleration before the Enlightenment* (Philadelphia: University of Pennsylvania Press, 1998), 4.
8. As described by his contemporary Johann Jakob Lerche, in Ioann-Iakub Lerkhe, "Prodolzhenie izvestiia o vtorom puteshestvii doktora i kollezhskaia sovetnika Lerkha

v Persiiu, 1746 po 1747 god.," *Novyia ezhemesiachnyia sochineniia* 63 (1791): 74.

9. Brief biographical information on Prince El'murza and his sons Devlet-Girei, Temir-Bulat, Inal, Mamet-Girei, and Kasbulat is in A. V. Kazakov, *Adygi (cherkesy) na rossiiskoi voennoi sluzhbe. Voevody i ofitsery. Seredina XVI – nachalo XX v.* (Nal'chik: El'-Fa, 2006), 77, 78–81, 85, 87–88.

10. Kazakov, *Adygi*, 78–79; Thomas Barrett, *At the Edge of Empire: The Terek Cossacks and the North Caucasus Frontier, 1700–1860* (Boulder: Westview Press, 1999), 35.

11. A record of the ranks and grants awarded to Kabardian and Kumyk notables in Russian service is in Arkhiv vneshnei politiki Rossiiskoi imperii (hereafter AVPRI), f. Kabardinskie dela, op. 115/1, 1759–1763, d. 5, ll. 70–76ob. For information pertaining to Shelokh Kasimov, see ibid., ll. 74–75ob.

12. Johann Anton Güldenstädt, *Reisen durch Russland und im Caucasischen Gebürge*, ed. P. S. Pallas, 2 vols. (St. Petersburg: Kayserl. Akademie der Wissenschaften, 1787–1791), 1: 177–81; more accessible is Iogann Anton Gil'denshtedt, *Puteshestvie po Kavkazu v 1770–1773 gg.*, ed. Iu. Iu. Karpov and trans. T. K. Shafranovskaia (St. Petersburg: Peterburgskoe Vostokovedenie, 2002), 26–28, 53–57; Barrett, *At the Edge of Empire*, 34.

13. Barrett, *At the Edge of Empire*, 36.

14. A register of fugitives arriving at Kizliar in 1763 was appended to a 30 January 1764 report of the Kizliar commandant to the College of Foreign Affairs, in Vakhtang Nikolaevich Gamrekeli, comp., *Dokumenty po vzaimootnosheniiam Gruzii s Severnym Kavkazom v XVIII v.* (Tbilisi: Metsniereba, 1968), no. 31, 146–52.

15. According to a register of fugitive arrivals in Kizliar for 1768, the formula appears to have been as follows: "*On obiazalsia zdes' zhit' vechno v poddanstve, obshche s okochenskimi tatarami v svoem makhometanskom zakone.*" The register is in Gamrekeli, *Dokumenty po vzaimootnosheniiam*, no. 46, 190.

16. Frauendorf to Astrakhan Governor Zhilin, 16 September 1759, AVPRI, f. Kabardinskie dela, op. 115/1, 1759–1763, d. 5, l. 7. On 30 December 1759, the College of Foreign Affairs (hereafter CFA) finally received a copy of this report via Astrakhan, in ibid., ll. 10–13.

17. Tsentral'nyi gosudarstvennyi arkhiv Respubliki Dagestana (hereafter TsGARD), f. Kizliarskii komendant, op. 1, 1762, d. 500, l. 34, as quoted in Irina Ivanovna Iakubova, *Severnyi Kavkaz v russkoi-turetskikh otnosheniiakh v 40–70-e gody XVIII veka* (Nal'chik: El'brus, 1993), 67.

18. TsGARD, f. Kizliarskii komendant, op. 1, 1762, d. 500, ll. 37, 38, 39, cited and discussed in Iakubova, *Severnyi Kavkaz*, 68.

19. Frauendorf to Zhilin, 16 September 1759, AVPRI, f. Kabardinskie dela, op. 115/1, 1759–1763, d. 5, ll. 7–9 ob.

20. CFA decree to Frauendorf, 29 February 1760, AVPRI, f. Kabardinskie dela, op. 115/, 1759–1763, d. 5, ll. 22–25 ob.

21. Islam is mentioned in Konchokin's 1759 petition to Frauendorf, in *Kabardino-russkie otnosheniia v XVI–XVIII vv.* (hereafter *KRO*), 2 vols (Moscow: Izdatel'stvo Akademii nauk SSSR, 1957), 2:201.

22. The following discussion is based on the Senate report in *KRO*, 2:218–20.
23. J. C. Hurewitz, ed., *The Middle East and North Africa in World Politics: A Documentary Record*, 2 vols. (New Haven: Yale University Press, 1975), 1:73.
24. AVPRI, f. Snosheniia Rossii s Turtsiei, op. 89/8, 1763, d. 333, ll. 65–66 ob.
25. AVPRI, f. Snosheniia Rossii s Turtsiei, op. 89/8, 1763, d. 333, l. 67ob.
26. Obreskov's memorandum and supporting documents are in AVPRI, f. Snosheniia Rossii s Turtsiei, op. 89/8, 1764, d. 355, ll. 73–90 (in Russian), and ll. 94–97 (Italian copy of the memorandum).
27. AVPRI, f. Snosheniia Rossii s Turtsiei, op. 89/8, 1764, d. 355, ll. 74–76 ob.
28. AVPRI, f. Snosheniia Rossii s Turtsiei, op. 89/8, 1764, d. 355, ll. 78–84 ob.
29. Ibid., ll. 84ob–85 ob.
30. Ibid., ll. 86–87 ob.
31. Obreskov and Councilor Levashov, 10 August 1764, AVPRI, f. Snosheniia Rossii s Turtsiei, op. 89/8, 1764, d. 355, ll. 64–67ob.
32. AVPRI, f. Kabardinskie dela, op. 115/1, 1763, d. 8, l. 1.
33. Imperial rescript to Medem, 5 Sept. 1774, "K istorii Kavkaza i Zakavkaz'ia," *Russkii arkhiv* no. 4 (1889): 559–60.
34. Ibid., 560–61.
35. On Medem's campaign of 1769–70, see the documents in *KRO*, 2: no. 207–10; see also Medem's report to the CFA, 18 Sept. 1770, AVPRI, f. Kabardinskie dela, op. 115/1, 1770, d. 3, ll. 1–8.
36. "K istorii Kavkaza," 561–62.
37. Catherine confirmed Potemkin's report on 5 May 1776, *Polnoe sobranie zakonov Rossiiskoi imperii: Poveleniem Gosudaria imperatora Nikolaia Pavlovicha sostavlennoe. Sobranie pervoe s 1649 po 12 dekabria 1825 goda*, 45 vols. (St. Petersburg: Tipografiia Vtorogo Otdeleniia Sobstvennoi Ego imperatorskogo Velichestva Kantselarii, 1830–1916), 20:374–75; the Senate gave its support to the plan in a 28 Oct. 1776 report to Catherine, in Rossiiskii gosudarstvennyi arkhiv drevnykh aktov (hereafter RGADA), f. 16, op. 1, d. 613, ch. 1, ll. 67–69 ob.
38. Iakobi to CFA, 19 Dec. 1777, *KRO*, 2: 324; Iakobi to Potemkin, 19 Dec. 1777, RGADA, f. 16, op. 1, d. 613, ch. 1, l. 253-53 ob; Iakobi to Potemkin, 18 Jan. 1778, Rossiiskii gosudarstvennyi voenno-istoricheskii arkhiv (hereafter RGVIA), f. 52, op. 1, d. 161, l. 3.
39. *PSZ*, 20: no. 14,464, 374; Petr Grigor'evich Butkov, *Materialy dlia novoi istorii Kavkaza s 1722 po 1803 god*, 3 Vols. (St. Petersburg: [Tipografiia Imperatorskogo Akademii nauk], 1869), 2:49.
40. Butkov, *Materialy*, 2:48.
41. A description of the proposed line between the Terek and Don Rivers was attached to Potemkin's report of 27 April 1777, *Sbornik Imperatorskago russkago istoricheskago obshchestva* (hereafter *SIRIO*), 148 vols. (St. Petersburg, 1867–1916), 145 (1914): 414–16.
42. In one report, he even claimed that Kabardians were grateful to Catherine for building

the new line; see Iakobi to CFA, 19 Dec. 1777, *KRO*, 2:324.
43. Iakobi to CFA, 19 Dec. 1777, *KRO*, 2:325.
44. Butkov, *Materialy*, 2:52–3.
45. Gustav Ernest von Strandman, "Zapiski Gustvava fon Shtrandmana," in Iakov A. Gordin, ed., *Kavkazskaia voina: istoki i nachalo, 1770–1820 gody* (St. Petersburg: Zhurnal "Zvezda," 2002), 25; Potemkin reported the order in a 28 Dec. 1779 letter to Catherine, RGVIA, f. 52, op. 1, d. 58, ch. 9, l. 65.
46. Iakobi to Potemkin, 8 May 1779, RGVIA, f. 52, op. 1, d. 183, ch. 3, l. 115.
47. Butkov, *Materialy*, 2:52–56.
48. Shtrandman, "Zapsiki," 29.
49. "Obligations imposed on Kabardian chiefs, nobles and all the people," December 1779, RGADA, f. 23, op. 1, d. 5, ch. 10, ll. 534–35 ob.
50. Butkov, *Materialy*, 2:59; Shtrandman, "Zapiski," 29.
51. RGADA, f. 23, op. 1, d. 5, ch. 10, ll. 536 ob, 537 ob.
52. Gudovich report of 7 Nov. and CFA rescript of 20 Nov. 1791, ibid., ll. 15ob–16, 1ob.
53. CFA to Gudovich, 22 Feb. 1792, ibid., l. 2–2ob; I. V. Gudovich, "Zapiska o sluzhbe general-fel'dmarshala grafa I. V. Gudovicha (im smamim sostavlennaia)," *Russkii vestnik* 1/1-3 (1, nos. 1–3?) (1841): 651.
54. Gudovich to CFA, 16 Jan. 1792, *Akty sobrannye Kavkazkoiu arkheograficheskoiu komissieiu* (hereafter *AKAK*) 12 vols. (Tbilisi: Tipografiia Kantselarii glavnonachal'stviushchego grazhdanskoi chast'iu na Kavkaze, 1866–1904), 2:1122–23.
55. Imperial decree, 28 Feb. 1792, in ibid., 1123–24; see also Gudovich to CFA, 24 March 1792, report, AVPRI, f. Snosheniia s Persiei, op. 77/1, 1791–96, d. 895, l. 17ob.
56. Imperial decree of 28 Feb. 1792, in *AKAK*, 2: 1123–24; CFA to Gudovich, 22 Feb. 1792, AVPRI, f. Snosheniia s Persiei, op. 77/1, 1791–96, d. 895, ll. 2ob–3ob.
57. Gudovich to Catherine, 12 Jan. 1793, RGADA, f. 23, op. 1, d. 37, ll. 40–43; see also Gudovich to CFA, 28 June 1793, AVPRI, f. Snosheniia s Persiei, op. 77/1, 1791–96, d. 895, l. 23–23ob.
58. Gudovich to CFA, 16 Nov. 1793, ibid., l. 25–25ob.
59. Gudovich to CFA, 23 Apr. 1794, ibid., l. 30.
60. Gudovich to CFA , 26 Feb. 1794, ibid., l. 29; CFA to Gudovich, 2 May 1794, ibid., l. 6. Gudovich estimated the cost of the fortifications at 141,866 rubles. Perhaps the desire to cut costs had something to do with the decision to call an end fort-building on the Line, much as it had in the decision to reduce by half (from twelve to six) the number of courts in Kabarda.
61. Gudovich to CFA, 26 Feb. 1794, AVPRI, f. Snosheniia s Persiei, op. 77/1, 1791–96, d. 895, l. 28.
62. Gudovich to CFA, 8 Aug. 1794, ibid., l. 31–31ob; Gudovich to Lt. Colonel Urakov (Russian bailiff among the Kabardians), 22 Sept. 1794, in *AKAK*, 2: 1127–28.
63. Gudovich to CFA, 9 Dec. 1794, AVPRI, f. Snosheniia s Persiei, op. 77/1, 1791–96, d. 895, l. 32.

64. *AKAK*, 2:1128.
65. Paul Dukes, ed. and trans., *Russia under Catherine the Great*, vol. 2, *Catherine the Great's Instruction (Nakaz) to the Legislative Commission, 1767* (Newtonville, MA: Oriental Research Partners, 1977), 104 (arts. 494–95).
66. Synod decree of 17 June 1773, *PSZ*, 19, no. 139996, 775–76.
67. Isabel de Madariaga, *Russia in the Age of Catherine the Great* (New Haven: Yale University Press, 1981), 503.
68. A. V. Khrapovitskii, *Dnevnik A. V. Khrapovitskago s 18 Ianvaria po 17 Sentiabria 1793 goda*, ed. Nikolai P. Barsukov (Moscow: Universitetskaia tipografiia, 1901), 2.
69. Mary Fulbrook, "Legitimation Crises and the early Modern State: The Politics of Religious Toleration," in *Religion and Society in Early Modern Europe 1500–1800*, ed. Kaspar von Greyerz (London: George Allen & Unwin, 1984), 155.
70. Benjamin J. Kaplan, *Divided by Faith: Religious Conflict and the Practice of Toleration in Early Modern Europe* (Cambridge: The Belknap Press of Harvard University Press, 2007), 8; on toleration as "a social practice," see also the essays in Greyerz, ed., *Religion and Society*, and John Christian Laursen and Cary J. Nederman, eds., *Beyond the Persecuting Society: Religious Toleration before the Enlightenment* (Philadelphia: University of Pennsylvania Press, 1998).
71. Kaplan, *Divided by Faith*, 8.
72. Alexandra Walsham, *Charitable Hatred: Tolerance and Intolerance in England, 1500–1700* (Manchester: Manchester University Press, 2006), 4.
73. This is true not only of Russian empire-building in eighteenth-century northern Caucasia. See, for example, Geraci and Khodarkovsky, eds., *Of Religion and Identity*; Irina Paert, *Old Believers, Religious Dissent, and Gender in Russia* (Manchester: Manchester University Press, 2003); Robert D. Crews, "Empire and the Confessional State: Islam and Religious Politics in Nineteenth-Century Russia," *American Historical Review* 108, no. 1 (2003): 50–83; idem, *For Prophet and Tsar*; Heather Coleman, *Russian Baptists and Spiritual Revolution* (Bloomington: Indiana University Press, 2005); Breyfogle, *Heretics and Colonizers*; Bobrovnikov, "Islam in the Russian Empire"; Darius Staliūnas, *Making Russians: Meaning and Practice of Russification in Lithuania and Belarus after 1863* (Amsterdam: Rodopi, 2007); Barbara Skinner, *The Western Front of the Eastern Church: Uniate and Orthodox Conflict in 18th-Century Poland, Ukraine, Belarus and Russia* (DeKalb: Northern Illinois University Press, 2009); Mikhail Dolbilov, *Russkii krai, chuzhaia vera: Etnoreligioznaia politika v Litve i Belorusii pri Aleksandre II* (Moscow: Novoe literaturnoe obozrenie, 2010); Aleksandr Polunov," Poniatiia *svoboda sovesti* i *veroterpimost'* v obshchestvenno-politicheskom diskurse Rossii kontsa XIX–nachala XX veka," in *"Poniatiia o Rossii": K istoricheskoi semantike imperskogo perioda*, ed. A. Miller, D. Sdvizhkov, and Ingrid Schirle, 2 vols. (Moscow: Novoe literaturnoe obozrenie, 2012), 1:559–73; and the articles by Gary M. Hamburg, Paul W. Werth, Victoria Frede, and Randall A. Poole in the forum "Religious Freedom and the Problem of Tolerance in Russian History," *Kritika: Explorations in Russian and Eurasian History* 13, no. 3 (Summer 2012): 509–634.
74. Laursen and Nederman, eds., *Beyond the Persecuting Society*, 2; Walsham, *Charitable Hatred*, 5.

Transcending Boundaries: When the Mamluk Legacy Meets a Family of Armeno-Georgian Interpreters*

HIROTAKE MAEDA

This article seeks to provide insight into the legacy of the Caucasus as a traditional supplier of human resources to the outside world. It sheds light on the experiences of those Caucasian peoples who left their homes and joined Middle Eastern societies. The first part of the article reveals the complicated nature of their self-perceptions. The second part investigates two examples of Caucasians who became part of a "foreign" elite, one in Iran and one in Egypt. The flexibility of their identities allowed them to transcend otherwise formidable cultural barriers and adapt socially in the nineteenth century, a period that witnessed rapid social changes. These cases of human mobility and cultural interrelations attest to the multilayered nature of Caucasian identity.

---

* I profoundly thank Prof. Grigol (Gia) Beradze of the Tsereteli Institute of Oriental Studies in Tbilisi for his regular consultations. This paper could not have been written had Grigol Beradze not suggested during my first stay in Georgia in 1995 that the most Georgian Mamluk ever was Ioseb Jughashvili, known as Stalin. Certainly if it were a great irony, I was struck by the complicated historical settings peoples of Caucasia had possessed. I am grateful to Tamaz Natroshvili for many interesting discussions on Georgian history. His articles and essays reflect well on the Georgian perception of their historical legacy, which Natroshvili describes with very beautiful touches.

Introduction

For centuries, Caucasian boys and girls, often prized for their beauty, were circulated throughout the Islamic Middle East as slaves. Slave trading was a most inhumane custom but it was also one of the most ancient and long-lived. Indeed, the trade of human beings in the Middle East flourished up until the mid-nineteenth century. In scale it rivaled the far better known slave trade across the Atlantic.

Slaves in Middle Eastern societies have long attracted scholars' attention as they not only colored the court life of Islamic empires but also supported ruling dynasties on many occasions, even providing military manpower. In the thirteenth century, Turkish and Caucasian slaves from the Qipchaq plain started to rule the whole of Egypt and led that land to prosperity. The famous Arab historian and social scientist Ibn Khaldun praised such Mamluk (meaning "those who are possessed" in Arabic) warriors, or so-called slave soldiers, for their contributions to protecting the "Islamic world" from the threat of the Mongols.[1] At the height of the Mamluk dynasty in Egypt, the leader of the country was elected from among liberated military slaves. Since the son of a Mamluk could never serve in the elite military corps, practically speaking only an imported (former) slave could become a sultan.[2]

The "Mamluk" theory crystalized by the late Prof. David Ayalon reflects partly a political wisdom in traditional Muslim discourse on community and polities. However, it also reflects a European historical narrative that dominated for centuries.[3] It should be pointed out that long before the modern era, when Europeans constructed an "Islamic" version of human slavery that developed into a distinct academic discourse with a slave soldier paradigm, many European observers had noted the political system of elite recruitment among slaves.

Scholars who were influenced directly or indirectly by European observations, attitudes, and values constructed this slave soldier paradigm. Many Europeans feared this means of forced recruitment of human resources and condemned it as cruel. Others, however, admired it, regarding it as a "liberating" tradition because slaves could become kings without a noble background, something that was unimaginable in contemporary Europe. These views reflect the complicated sentiments of Europeans towards "Islamic

Bridge at Yerevan

society." It should be pointed out that these opposing views proceed from the same roots of distinguishing oneself by praise or casting blame. Later, "progressive" Europeans expressed ambiguous attitudes towards "Oriental" practices, either disregarding them or rather indulging in romanticism. Considering the "Islamic" practices positively or negatively, their observations exercised a certain influence on the studies of Islamic "slave soldiers."[4]

Caucasians, who were common victims of the slave trade, were not only evaluated by their beauty and their status as slaves. The essence of slave soldiers is a function of not just their slave status but also their outsider status, their "foreignness" to the existing state elite and local organs. Their status as slaves and their physical appearance were only elements of this condition. In the pre-modern period, many ruling dynasties tried to consolidate their power by introducing foreign elements into the core of ruling institutions. This tendency to emphasize the separation of ruled and ruling matched the tradition of recruiting ruling elites from the outside.

The foreign origins of the slave king would be effectively exploited in multi-ethnic and religious Middle Eastern societies. Modern studies, however, have intentionally ignored the multi-dimensional character of their identity. Instead, the social and psychological transformation of their identity was usually stressed for explaining the strength of these foreign elites. In this regard Marshall Hodgson had already insisted that "it would be hard to place such peoples as Georgians and Armenians unequivocally within any one major "civilization."[5] The following study will provide a nuanced picture of the life story of "slave elites" from the Caucasus. It will pay special attention to the perceptions local Caucasians had of those who migrated to "foreign lands."

Images of the Self among Caucasians

It should be mentioned that Caucasians have accepted the dominant European discourse of slave soldiers' doctrine, albeit with their own interpretations. Consider, for example, a masterpiece of Georgian film, *The Mamluk* (by David Rondli in 1958, *Mamluki* in Georgian). This film vividly reflects the "Georgian perspective," one greatly influenced by European academic discourse and Soviet "national" sentiment alike. Two Georgians soldiers, Khvicha and Gocha, were fiercely fighting each other to the death on Egyptian soil. They were in a foreign land far away from their homeland. One, Khvicha, was a leader of a Mamluk corps and the other, Gocha, was a military officer of a Napoleonic army. The narrator stresses that this "cursed fate" was not rare for these "excellent children" of Georgia of that time. The film depicts both the Georgian imagery and perceptions of Oriental barbarism and European colonialism and aggression that had been accepted and expressed in 1950 s.

During the battle, Khvicha, the Egyptian hero of Georgian origin, realized that Gocha, the European commander, was his childhood friend with whom he had been kidnapped in a village in western Georgia. He successfully recognized his friend, however, only during his death. The last word Khvicha had heard Gocha utter was "*deda*," which means "mother" in Georgian. When the two heroes tragically collapse one after the other in the desert, the narrator proclaims that "they are the sons of Georgia." They could have contributed to their Georgian motherland; instead, they died practicing foreign religions and customs as victims of Oriental and Western absolutism.

Although the film is very dramatic and is sophisticated beyond the simply national, in this romantic image of a nation that it paints we see the same one-sided vision at the heart of the slave soldier doctrine that distinguishes inside and outside. It is important to note that the nineteenth-century romantic, patriotic writer Vazha-Pshavela (Luka Razikashvili, 1861–1915) recognized a fragile reality when he openly expressed the paradoxical relations (though based on a very romantic and "patriotic" view).

In his *From the East to the West (mashrikit maghrebamde)* published in 1991, Tamaz Natroshvili, a Georgian scholar of Oriental studies, well illustrates the ambiguous view of Vazha-Pshavela, a "national" writer, on Giorgi Saakadze (d. 1629), another prominent figure of Georgian history.[6] Before *The Mamluk* was screened in the 1950s, the life of Saakadze was made into a film in the midst of World War II. Saakadze was a famous Georgian general of the early seventeenth century who led a general uprising in eastern Georgia against the Safavid shah 'Abbas I (r. 1587–1629).[7] This national hero, however, had earlier been a close and faithful servant of Shah 'Abbas before the revolt and supported his lord on many military operations. The author (Natroshvili) shared the same pain as Vazha-Pshavela in that the terrible fate of the sons of Georgia consisted not only in their being in a foreign land but also in their association with a different homeland.

Interestingly, Girogi Saakadze was hailed as a national hero in Stalin's era, while Stalin himself questioned Vaja Pshavela's genius.[8] Soviet authorities, especially during World War II, praised Saakadze as a "national hero" who fought desperately against the enemy inside Georgia, the "great nobles," and outside Georgia, the Muslim "tyrannies" of Turkey and Persia. The ambivalent "patriotic view" that had existed before Soviet times was denied by "universal revolutionists." The characterization of Stalin, Pshavela, and Saakadze, the complicated triangle of outstanding Georgian historical figures, each carries contradictory "national" sentiments.[9]

We notice that the Caucasian perception of the "Islamic slave institution" and its "victims" were neither singular nor dichotomous like Europe and Asia even if influenced by the dominant European discourse on the Islamic Middle East as well as by modern national sentiments of the Soviet type. These outsider elites who belonged to or were connected with a wider community of Caucasian migrants were experiencing their ancestors' fates, whether bitter or sweet, as their own. In the following, we investigate several cases of Caucasians' migration to the Middle East in the early modern period in order to better understand Caucasian identity.

Caucasian "Slaves" in Iran in the Early Modern Age

Safavid System of Foreign Elites

Although scarcely researched, the Iranian case provides ample evidence for reconsidering the "slave soldier paradigm." Safavid slave soldiers or *ghulam*s possessed distinctive features that reflected the accepted theory of Islamic military slavery. Vertically, the institution was a fusion of the local ruling system and Safavid elite culture. As opposed to the slave soldier doctrine, the double identity of the Caucasian servants of the Safavid dynasty was not an exceptional case.[10] Safavid policy avoided relying too much on one element of society, especially Turkish and Iranian elements, and encouraged the integration of Caucasians into its political system and culture. Caucasian elites were brought into imperial household institutions, but because the process of integration was coercive, it often spurred the Caucasians to "awaken" and interrogate their own identity, even as they remained politically loyal to the imperial order.

In these circumstances, towards the end of the dynasty even the royal Bagratid princes played a significant role in the Safavid political arena. Ironically they took over key administrative and military posts in an empire that had, in many cases, been occupied by powerful *ghulam* families before.[11] The last Safavid governor of Qandahar (a key city uniting Khorasan in eastern Iran and India, now situated in Afghanistan) was Gurgin Khan, a Georgian prince of the Kartli branch, who reigned from 1703 to 1709. Simultaneously he was a king of the Kartli kingdom of eastern Georgia as Giorgi XI (r. 1676–88, 1703–09).

When Georgian princes were murdered in Qandahar and the Safavid monarch lost his function as a mediator and protector of the imperial order, that order easily dissolved in the face of the military challenge of Afghans from the southwestern frontier who sacked the imperial capital Isfahan in 1722. At the same time, this incident triggered a fierce struggle among their Caucasian subjects since the loss of the imperial center meant the delicate and complicated balances of regional powers constructed under the Safavid hegemony were lost.[12]

The collapse of Safavid rule also caused a wave of migrations to the neighboring polities which later impacted the wider region, including Georgia. King Vakhtang VI, nephew of the above-mentioned Gurgin, fled to Russia with his entourage of some 1,200 persons. Thus was the born the prospect of Georgians becoming Russian subjects. The ancestor of the first de facto governor of Georgia, General Petre Tsitsianov was among them. Politically as well, the collapse of Safavid rule allowed Russia to project influence into the South Caucasus in a serious way, this being the first significant appearance of Russia into south of the Caucasus.

From Nadir Shah to Naserodin Shah

There are numerous studies on Nadir Shah's Caucasian connections, although they are scattered in the national narrative. In his time there was already a "shuttle" route between the Caucasus and Iran as the region was still integrated in Iranian or Ottoman politics, but Russia was already attracting many Caucasians, especially in the second half of the eighteenth century.

The story of the ancestors of a famous Russian general illustrates this complex flow of people. The hero of the war with Napoleon (known to Russians as the Great Patriotic War of 1812), Petre Bagration (1765–1812), was a great grandson of King Iese of Kartli (1680/81?–1727, r. 1714–16), half-brother of King Vakhtang VI. Iese was also known as Aliquli Khan when he was under Iranian patronage and as Mustafa Pasha when he was under Ottoman patronage. Iese began his early career as a Safavid military commander. He fought with the Afghans in southeast Iran alongside his uncle Gurgin/Girogi XI and half-brother Kaykhosrow. After the death of Kaykhosrow, he was appointed governor of Kerman then *tupchibashi* (commander of the ancillary forces). He was sent to Kartli as a *vali*-king in 1714, but his half-brother Vakhtang agreed to become Muslim and was then given rulership of Kartli in 1716. Iese was temporally in custody in Tbilisi where his nephew Bakar, a son of Vakhtang IV and acting governor, ruled. Iese reverted to Christianity at that time and in 1721 started serving Vakhtang, who had returned from Iran. After the migration of Vakhtang VI and his subjects to Russia, Iese reconverted to Islam in 1724, this time to the Sunni faith and ruled Tbilisi under Ottoman hegemony.[13]

In spite of all these endeavors Iese's descendants could not find suitable positions in Georgia. The above-mentioned Russian general Petre was born in Qizlari, a Russian stronghold in the northern Caucasus where his grandfather Aleksandre had immigrated in 1759 in pursuit of Russian aid.[14] In his letter to Queen Elizaveta I in April 1759, Aleksandre wrote, "When my father, King Iese, was in Persia for a time at the shah's court, I was left to live there in the capital of Isfahan by King Iese, who then left, and I remained there with my mother at the shah's court where I was raised in their profane and abominable Mohammedan faith"[15] He continued to serve the Persian court and Nadir Shah gave him a salary and land. Aleksandre, however, went to Georgia where his full brother remained. His brother, who later became the archbishop (*arkhiepiskopos*) of Volodimerskii, baptized his whole family.[16] In the petition, the author inadvertently reveals how much their complex cultural and religious background was influenced by the political realities surrounding the Caucasus region.

In these fragile and complicated international circumstances, Georgian principalities experienced great difficulties in maintaining their semi-independent status. As a result, the role of "diplomacy" became much more important. Exactly around this period, members of an Armenian family serving Georgian kings deliberately enlarged their activities utilizing their traditional knowledge.

A Translator Became a Mamluk

The History of the Enikolopians

This Armenian family bore a strange name, the Enikolopeantz (hereafter Enikolopians),[17] which means "language box" in Georgian. The first reference to this family occurs in 1688, the same year the Safavid shah Soleyman I (r. 1666–94) appointed a Russian-bred Kakhetian prince, Erekle, as *vali* (governor) of the Kartli kingdom/province, thus terminating the traditional pro-Kartli policy that had lasted more than a century. The Enikolopians started their service and became important court officials in these circumstances.[18]

The first two representatives of this family are recorded as librarians of the Georgian court. In the Middle East, translators played an important role serving not only as bureaucrats but also as intermediaries with minority subjects, such as the Phanariot Greeks in the Ottoman Empire. In Georgia, Armenians produced important intellectuals and courtiers, including the Tumanishivilis/Tumanovs.[19] By serving as cultural middlemen, the Enikolopians became influential courtiers, and from this family Gurgin Khan played the important role of a diplomat who shuttled between the Ottoman and Iranian courts in the second half of the eighteenth century.[20]

Mirza Rostom's Life

After the Russian Empire's annexation of eastern Georgia (Kartli-Kakheti kingdom) by the Russian Empire in 1801, Gurgin's third son Abram became a Russian subject and continued working as interpreter until his death in 1836 (his namesake grandson became the brother-in-law of Mikhail

An Armenian and a Georgian

Loris-Melikov, a well-known politician in the Russian empire during the reign of Aleksandr II). However, Mirza Rostom, the second son, chose a different life and master by entering into the service of the Qajar shahs in Iran.

Rostom's life before departing for Iran was filled with travel. According to the anonymous Georgian genealogy, Rostom started to work as a servant of the Georgian court and made the close acquaintance of Prince Valerian Zubov (1771–1804), a famous Russian commander who was a guest of

Erekle II. When King Erekle II (r. 1744–98) deprived the Enikolopians of their lands, Rostom went to Austria where he was said to have studied in a newly established military school. After learning about the changed situation in his homeland, Rostom returned to Georgia in 1805 or 1806.

In Georgia Rostom was told that his two younger half-brothers Jhan-Bashkh and Jhangir had been lost in Aqa Muhammad's invasion in 1795. The only surviving brother, Chongur (later Manuchihr), was also taken captive on the banks of the Aparan River near Yerevan while accompanying the campaign of General Tsitsianov (1754–1806) in the summer of 1804. Rostom decided to bring his brother back for his mother-in-law Voskum Khanum.[21]

Mirza Rostom was informed that captives at Aparan had been brought to Tabriz. Rostom knew the fate of his brother in Tabriz where the now-converted Manuchihr (Chongur) had been made a eunuch and was attached to a harem in Tehran. Rostom could not trace the fate of his other two younger brothers in Tabriz and decided to go to Tehran to bring Manuchihr back. Crown Prince Abbas Mirza, crown prince and ruler of Azerbaijan, wanted Rostom to contribute to the military reform and gave Rostom a horse and twenty *toman* for the journey.

With the help of Tbilisi's Armenians who were active in Tehran, Rostom sought the emancipation of his brother, but he failed. Rostom was introduced to the court as a military reform specialist. He was ordered to prepare ten young men, and the shah himself often went to watch the men train in the square. Rostom stayed in Tehran for a month and twice had the chance to ask the shah to emancipate Manuchihr. However, the shah did not agree. Manuchihr Khan Mutamed al-Doule went on to become one of the most influential courtiers serving the Qajar shahs in the first half of nineteenth century. Rostom had promised to go back to Tabriz when Abbas Mirza helped him. Abbas Mirza now gave him fifty young men from good families for training. After the arrival of French military advisors, Rostom became an advisor in the diplomatic field for Abbas Mirza.[22]

It is important to note that Mirza Rostom played an intermediary role between Abbas Mirza and the Armenian Catholicos in Echimiajin, too. The Armenians were apparently confused by the new situation, and when they selected a Russian subject Eferem as the new head of the Catholicate in January 1809, they asked Mirza Rostom to obtain the order (*farman*) of

Abbas Mirza. They expressed in a letter that they had been under Persian protection for fifteen hundred years. Rostom made every effort to maintain good relations with Abbas Mirza and on the recommendation of Abbas Mirza married Nazlu Shahbazean, who was from a local Armenian family. Thus, the crown prince also tried to fortify his Armenian connections. Shermazanian surmised that Rostom died before 1812.[23]

For all intents and purposes Rostom was a secretary of Abbas Mirza, using his knowledge as a scribe and multiligual talent inherited and received as a member of the Enikolopians. After Rostom's death, his younger brother Aghalo Khan seems to have thrived in his role as a servant of Abbas Mirza and as a mediator between Echimiajin and the Iranian court[24]. Rostom's brothers and sons were among the most powerful and successful courters in first half of the nineteenth century and played a significant role in Qajar politics. His son Solomon was first trained in the Russian army and then went to Iran. His elder brother and the namesake of his grandfather Gurgin became a governor of Isfahan. His sons Nariman and Jangir (Jahangir) both became influential diplomats and administrators in the reign of Naserodin Shah. If we take the "Mamluks" as military-bureaucrat elites of Muslim empires of foreign origin, an Armenian family of interpreter-diplomats produced "Mamluks" in the nineteenth century.[25]

Pre and Early Modern Caucasian "Slaves" in Egypt

The Caucasians' role in Egypt is well-known for the later Mamluk dynasty, and it is oftentimes even called the era of "Circassians." Knowledge of their interrelations with their homeland is scarce; however, surviving sources allow us some insights. One of the best-known Mamluk sultans, Barquq (r. 1382–89, 1390–99), was originally from the Kasa tribe of the Circassians and arrived in Egypt as a slave from Crimea. This famous Mamluk sultan, who was called "the founder of Circassian rule," was visited by his father Anas when he became sultan.[26] The Mamluk sultan Inal was referred to as the ancestor of the distinguished Circassian noble family Cherkasskii. In this way they proclaimed their ties to the "homeland."[27]

In the eighteenth century, we find occasional details of Caucasian Mamluks' connections with their homeland, though in some cases the descriptions maintain the literary form of relating a legend. Baghdad was in the hands of Georgian Mamluks mostly throughout the eighteenth century and early nineteenth century.[28] The original family name of two distinguished commanders, Davud Pasha in Baghdad and Ibrahim Pasha in Cairo, are known in modern Georgian historiography.[29] Both had close contact with their homeland.

Recently Daniel Crecelius and Gotcha Djaparidze made important studies on these "Mamluk" elements of Georgian origin.[30] Ibrahim Shinjikashivili sent money to his native village through his brother and brother-in-law, who visited him in Egypt in 1778. A few years later, in 1786 there were series of diplomatic missions visiting Cairo from the Georgian king and Russian Tsar separately. Ibrahim Bey showed an inclination towards Russian authority.[31] Dr. Djaparidze's long durée study itself deserves scholarly attention in terms of the geo-political perception of Caucasian locals. During his visit to Matrqopi with the intention of finding the successors of Ibrahim Pasha's relatives in 1963, Djaparidze met two Shinjikashvilis who told him that the village tower was built with money sent from "Misr" by a person belonging to the same clan. Then, the old man did not know where "Misr" was.[32] Of course, Misr means Egypt in Arabic (today as well). Accepting a western map of the world, Georgians forgot the word Misr. The name "Egypt" represents a somehow strange, hybrid combination of antiquity and modernity in this case, and it resembles to some extent the naming of the "Caucasus".

Djaparidze has already shown that a relative of Ibrahim Pasha in Cairo made a petition to the Georgian king and insisted that the Georgian authorities issue a decree granting his brother in Georgia freeman status unless he would be forced to leave the homeland.[33] A petition for the division of the Marghishvili family is recorded. Ivane and Aber Marghishvili asked Erekle II to order their master Zurab Tumanishvili to honor the provisions of the petition. The brothers divided their family property with another brother Iese who had been in Egypt (Misr) as a captive and had returned.[34] In the course of the nineteenth century slave trading gradually declined, but we find a lasting impact of the "Mamluk" tradition.

A Mamluk Became a Translator

The Last Mamluk

In 1812, in a village of the Lanchkhuti region of the Guria province of western Georgia, the eight-year-old son of Lazare Tsilosani was kidnapped when his family was attacked by his countrymen. First, the raiders kept the young Ioseb Tsilosani in Poti's fortress on the Black Sea coast and later sold him with a boy from Mingrelia (Samegrelo) to Hasan Agha Mseroghli[35], a famous slave trader from Hopa (Today situated at the border of Turkey and Georgia, Khopa in Georgian). Hasan Agha at that time was in western Georgia seeking Georgian boys and girls for the Ottoman sultan. The Georgian boys were then taken to Egypt and Mirakhor-Mohamed Agha, an influential retainer of Muhammad Ali, became their master. It should be noted that although in 1811, the year before Ioseb was kidnapped, Muhammad Ali had slaughtered Mamluk elements in Egypt, the traditional movement of peoples had never stopped.[36]

Now a Mamluk, Ioseb was renamed Ali Amedi and converted to Islam. He studied Ottoman Turkish and Arabic as well as the Qur'an under two teachers for four or five years. In 1818 he was freed by his master Mirakhor-Mohamed Agha and together with another slave, Hasan Selim, was named as a potential successor to his patron's estates after Mirakhor-Mohamed's only daughter Seit-Zeinab. In 1821 the ruler of Egypt Muhammad Ali ordered Ali Amedi and Hasan Selim to receive military education at Qasr al-'Ayni. After finishing school in 1823 he was ordered to study the Italian language. Then in 1825–26 the Egyptian government sent him and Hasan Selim to Paris for the purpose of receiving a higher education. After learning French, Ali Amedi hoped to specialize in painting but was ordered to pursue engineering. He finished the course in four years in 1831–1832.

During that time, Ali Amedi learned of the death of his patron in Egypt. He claimed he was named to marry Sait-Zeinab, his patron's sole daughter, but there is no evidence that he ever married her. When he left Paris he went to the Russian consulate in Istanbul. There he pledged allegiance to the Russian tsar Nikolai I in a letter written in French and Arabic. He reclaimed his original name of Ioseb Tsilosani and on November 2, 1832, began a position at the chancellery of Baron Grigorii Vladimirovich Rozen

(Georg Andreas von Rosen), chief administrator of Caucasia in Tbilisi. He never became a "Mamluk" in Egypt in the narrow sense of the word, but his career as a member of the state elite of "foreign origin" followed the traditional pattern of a Mamluk. It attests further to the fact that the Mamluk system was a system where children of "foreign" origin were brought up as "state servants" before the age of nations. Now, Tsilosani returned to his motherland, became a military officer, and later worked for the Russian state as a translator. He looked for his immediate family members, but his search was in vain. Since we do have a photo from 1858 or 1859 showing Tsilosani's son Niko with his "cousin" Levan Tsilosani, we can safely assume that he later successfully made contact with his extended family.

After Tsilosani's Return

It is interesting to note that Tsilosani's knowledge of Arabic and French affected his fate after he returned to his "homeland," although not on a practical political level. We should remember that Russia had long ago already formed her foreign policy towards the Ottomans. With Egypt's Muhammad Ali and his armies challenging the Ottoman sultan for regional supremacy, Egyptian-Ottoman relations were perhaps one of the most important international issues at the time. Nonetheless, Tsilosani was sent to the Northwestern Caucasian front on the Black Sea coast in 1837 (Needless to say his knowledge of Ottoman Turkish should have been in consideration for this task but his activity was limited to a local Caucasian level, not an imperial one like diplomacy).[37]

On a personal level, however, he never forgot his early life in Egypt. Indeed, his stint in Egypt continued to influence his career throughout his life, even though he was not directly involved in diplomacy. In 1839, having learned of the death of his formal owner's daughter Seit-Zeinab, Tsilosani appealed to the Egyptian court to take control of his former master's property. He claimed to have been named successor of the property by his deceased master together with his colleague Hasan Selim. He insisted that Egyptian authorities had confirmed his right to succession during his stay in Egypt, and there had been no incident whereby this decision had ever been annulled. He even appealed to the Foreign Ministry of the Russian Empire to protect his right to succession.

Mingrelian Wine Jar

At first Tsilosani wrote to Hasan Selim to ask for help to solve the issue and divide the property together according to their former master's will (Interestingly, he said that if Selim should send a letter to Tsilosani, he would pass along Selim's news to his relatives in Georgia). He received no reply, so again he sent an official petition to Cairo on June 24 of the same year. Eventually he received an official reply from Egyptian religious authorities, who refused his request on account of his conversion to Christianity. Hasan Selim (Selim Efendi) had been working in a language school at that time. He acknowledged that the property of his former patron was inherited by his slaves after the death of Seit-Zeinab but insisted that Tsilosani was not the only one slave but that there were five other slaves who also had a right to inherit the property. According to Hasan Selim, it was impossible to sell the waqf property and send a part of money to Tsilosani.

In 1840–41, Tsilosani married Epemia, daughter of the Armenian *dekanozi* Nikoloz Izmirov. The marriage, it appears, provided him a material base for he seemed to quit requesting his right for the property in Egypt In 1845–47 when Vorontsov became the Caucasian viceroy, Tsilosani continued to work in the army but was once ordered to visit Trabzon to translate documents from Ottoman Turkish into Russian. Later in 1854 he was temporarily commissioned to translate Turkish and Arabic documents preserved in Georgian churches. He retired from the viceroy's office on June 18, 1848. Thereafter, he concentrated on his literary activities. His first publication appeared in 1856 and was titled *New Dialogues of the Russians, French, Turkish, and Tatars with pronunciation of the two latter in Russian, divided into 130 parts for the young and those starting to learn Oriental languages*. This book consists of six hundred and seven pages. In 1862, he published a collection of proverbs in Arabic Turkish and Persian accompanied by translations into Russian. He also left an unpublished manuscript, *Dialogues in French and Arabic: Exercises for understanding the spoken Arabic language*.[38]

In light of his transregional and transimperial career, we would like to know more about his perception of national consciousness, but we have few materials to consult. He proclaimed that a reason for his return was his wish to return to his native Christianity. Judging from his activities, he prioritized a pragmatic way of life as a former "Mamluk" serving the Russian empire and did not emphasize any "Georgian-ness." Of course, this does not mean he lacked a consciousness of his national belongings. Here we should note that Tsilosani was acquainted with the famous French scholar of the Caucasus, Marie-Felicte Brosset. Moreover, his son Niko (1847–93) served as a Tsarist military officer and later became a renowned Georgian specialist of archeology. Tsilosani's direct line disappeared when his namesake grandson Ioseb (Soso) Tsilosani (1891–1917) died on March 7, 1917, during a battle with the Ottomans on the Caucasian front. Thus, the family's fate is connected with the military history of the Russian Empire towards the south.

Conclusion

The Caucasus has always been a borderland of great civilizations. We tend, naturally, to pay much attention to the influence of those "superior" entities. The scholarly literature on Mamluk institutions reflects this. However, if we think of the interrelations these Caucasian "slave solders" had with their homelands, a "Caucasian gravity" appears. Their in-betweeness and multiple identities are central features of the Caucasian historical experience.

For too long a time, insufficient attention has been paid to the fates of these trans-bordering elites. The reversed lives of the Caucasians I introduced in this paper were mostly neglected in Soviet "national" historiography and European Orientalism. In the pre-modern period, multiple identities and flexible social networks much connected through kin and other relations could set the trajectory for social activities. The Enikolopians' experience shows that identity was not merely "national" character but above all a reflection of the family's social status and the traditional capital they inherited from ancestors.

Interestingly, both cases connect with the profession of interpreter, a quintessential cultural middleman. Their cross-cultural character enabled their intermediary role especially in terms of economics and politics. Both cases in this paper show the acquisition and deployment of knowledge gained from different worlds. In this sense, at least in the first half of nineteenth century, the cross-cultural framework did not seem to change.

The question remains to what extent the Imperial authorities appreciated their "multiple identities." Meanwhile the self-configuration relying on "national identities" was just underway in Caucasian society in the late nineteenth century. It was a period of massive social transition. As means of transportation and communication rapidly developed and expanded, real political boundaries paradoxically appeared. In these circumstances, a translator could become a Mamluk and a Mamluk could become a translator.[39]

The fates of the Caucasians discussed herein was partly the legacy of Mamluk institutions and partly a reflection of the changes reshaping the Caucasus. By the end of the century, humans had become subject to scientific classification. At the same time, humans adopted or were assigned discrete national identities. Nations were "awakened" and created. The role of "foreign" elites and "foreign" communities started to decline as they were excluded from the "host societies." However, as such, their lives have a meaning when we consider the pre-national and national divide as well as the post-national society that would come.

Needless to say, the new reality brought about by the radical social changes of the nineteenth century awaits more elaborate study. How these flows of peoples affected their collective identities would be a new subject requiring its own study.

Notes

1. David Ayalon, "Mamlukiyyat," *Jerusalem Studies in Arabic and Islam* 2 (1980): 345, cited from *Outsiders in the Lands of Islam: Mamluks, Mongols and Eunuchs* (London: Variorum Reprints, 1988).
2. However, already from the late 1990's the segregation of the Mamluk corps was coming under question. See Thomas Philipp and Ulrich Haarmann, eds., *The Mamluks in Egyptian Politics and Society* (Cambridge: Cambridge University Press, 1998).
3. In the *Encyclopedia of Islam* Europeans' travel accounts were also used to explain "Islamic slavery" and its military institution, see C. E. Bosworth's article on *ghulam*s. C. E. Bosworth, "Ghulam. ii-Persia," *The Encyclopaedia of Islam*, New Edition, vol. II (Leiden-London 1965), 1081-84.
4. The perceived image of these Mamluk/Ghulam elements as absolute slaves fully devoted to their masters remains to this day. Recent studies, however, confirm the variety of their existences in various polities and regions. See the recent studies of Richard Eaton, Matthew Gordon, Jane Hathaway, and Eric R. Dursteler. I plan to discuss the issue of the paradigm in the introduction of a future publication on the Safavid royal *ghulam*s.

5. Marshall G. S. Hodgson, *Rethinking World History: Essays on Europe, Islam and World History* (Cambridge: Cambridge University Press, 1993), 84.
6. Tamaz Natroshvili, "Ori Mouravi" *Tseli erti da atasi* (Tbilisi: Merani, 1988). The general uprising is termed Matqopi's revolt/*martqopis ajanqeba* in Georgian history.
7. Shah Abbas I was the fifth shah of the Safavid dynasty. He brought the Safavids prosperity but at the price of his cruel policy towards the peripheries with successive slaughters and forced migrations. His endless effort to reconstruct the state structure produced contradictory historical phenomena, for Caucasians greatly contributed to building 'Abbas's empire based on the household institution (I temporary call it a "household empire," but they also became the direct victims of this policy. See Hirotake Maeda, "Exploitation of the Frontier: The Caucasus Policy of Shah 'Abbas I," in *Iran and the World in the Safavid Age*, ed. Willem Floor and Edmund Herzig, 471–89 (London: I. B. Tauris, 2012).
8. Tamaz Natroshvili, "Enas gitsunebt, Pshavelo…," *Akhsovda tu ara Sakartvelo* (Tbilisi: Damani, 1994). This book was dedicated to the most famous Georgian politician—Ioseb Jughashvili—known as Stalin. The book's title means "Remember Georgia or not."
9. Scholars of various fields have revealed the existence of a unique "Georgian modernity" and demonstrated its viability from the cross-cultural perspectives. See the works of Harsha Ram, Paul Manning, Austin Jersild, and others.
10. On the Safavid *Ghulam*s, see Hirotake Maeda, "On the Ethno-Social Background of Four *Gholām* Families from Georgia in Safavid Iran," *Studia Iranica* 32 (2003): 243–78; and Hirotake Maeda, "The Household of Allāhverdī Khān: An Example of Patronage Network in Safavid Iran," in *Géorgie entre Perse et Europe*, ed. Florence Hellot-Bellier and Iréne Natchkebia, 149–70 (Paris-Tbilissi: l'Harmattan, 2009). Also see the articles by Giorgio Rota.
11. On the active participation of Georgian princes in Safavid politics, see David Marshall Lang, *The Last Years of the Georgian Monarchy 1658–1832* (New York: Columbia University Press, 1957). Not only the Georgians but also Daghestan princes were active. Rudolf Matthee, "Blinded by Power: The Rise and Fall of Fath 'Ali Khan Daghestani, Grand Vizier under Shah Soltan Hoseyn Safavi (1127/1715–1133/1720)," *Studia Iranica* 33, no. 2 (2004): 179–220.
12. On Safavid-Georgian relations, see Hirotake Maeda, "Slave Elites Who Returned Home: Georgian Vālī-king Rostom and the Safavid Household Empire," *Memoirs of the Research Department of the Toyo Bunko* 69 (2011), 97–127; and Hirotake Maeda, "Parsadan Gorgijanidze's Exile in Shushtar: A Biographical Episode of a Georgian Official in the Service of the Safavids," *Journal of Persianate Studies* 1, no. 2 (2008): 218–29.
13. V. Gucua, "Iese, Aliquli-Khani," *Kartuli Sabchota Entsiklopedia* (1980), 5:88.
14. N. Nakashidze, "Bagrationi Petre Ivanes dze," *Kartuli Sabchota Entsiklopedia* (1977), 2:131.
15. Sean M. Pollock, "'As One Russian to Another': Prince Petr Ivanovich Bagration's Assimilation of Russian Ways," *Ab Imperio* no. 4 (2010): 113.
16. Iase Tsintsadze, "Ramdenime akhali tsnoba XVIII saukunis kartlis istoriisatvis," *Masalebi Sakartvelos da Kavkasiis istoriisatvis* 1942, part. 4 (Tbilisi: Sakartvelos ssr metsnierebata academia): 1–26 (especially 23–26).

17. In a work scheduled to be published by Yale University Press I plan to contribute a detailed article on this family. I discussed the interesting history of this family in several presentations, including "From 'Oriental' to 'Russian': Lives of One Armenian Noble Family in Tbilisi," part of the panel "Imperial Subjects and Cross-Cultural Contacts at the Border: Reconfiguration of Self in 19th–20th Century Caucasus and Volga-Ural," AAASS 39th National Convention, New Orleans, November 15, 2007.
18. D. Kldiashvili and M. Surguladze, eds., *Pirt'a anotirebuli lek'sikoni (XI–XVII ss.): K'art'uli istoriuli sabut'ebis mikhedvit'* (T'bilisi : Mec'niereba, 1991–93), 2: 133–34. Bejan Enakolopashvili was mentioned during 1688–93 as secretary-librarian (*mdivan-mtsignobari*) of Nazar-'Ali Khan (Erekle's name after conversion to Islam) and Paremuz Enakolopashvili during 1696–99 in the same post.
19. Not only did they play an intermediary role, but they also contributed to Georgian self-identity as the closest other. On their role, see Thornike Gordadze, "Formation socio-historique de la nation géorgienne: le legs des identités pré-modernes, les idéologies et acteurs nationalists" (PhD diss., Instituts d'études politiques, Paris, 2006).
20. On the lives of interpreters as transmitter of languages and cultures, see Frances E. Karttunen, *Between Worlds: Interpreters, Guides, and Survivors* (New Brunswick, NJ: Rutgers University Press, 1994).
21. The Georgian genealogy is by the unknown author: Galust Shermazanean, *Nivter azgayin patmutean hamar: yereveli hayikazunk i Parskastan (Materials for the National History: Distinguished Armenians in Persia)* (Rostov, 1890), 202–3. Shemazanian suggested Rostom's departure to Austria happened before 1795 but Prince Zubov's expedition was in 1796. The last Georgian king of the Kartli-Kakheti kingdom, Giorgi XII issued a Persian charter to the Enikolopians in September-October 1798. The Georgian king ordered that the Muslim and Christian populations of Ḥalvābār (Avlabari) be assigned to Mirza Ibrahim (Abraham) and Mirza Rustam (Rostom). The Central Historical Archive of Georgia 1450-57-21: 20b. So far we have no other materials to fix the date of Rostom's departure to Austria and, in general, his early life.
22. In fact, several of Napoleon's emissaries trained the army of Abbas Mirza in 1805–1807. Muriel Atkin, *Russia and Iran, 1780–1828* (Minneapolis: University of Minnesota Press, 1980), 126.
23. Shermazanian, *Nivter azgayin patmutean hamar*, 203–8. His younger brother Aghalo Khan seems to have succeeded him as a servant of Abbas Mirza and mediator between Echmiadzin and the Iranian court. He was charged with defending the Armenian population in the Ottoman-Iranian war in 1820–21. Enikolopov, "Griboedo i sem'ya Enikolopovykh," 82.
24. Aghalo was charged with defending the Armenian population in the Ottoman-Iranian war in 1820–21. Enikolopov, I., "Griboedov i sem'ya Enikolopovykh: k 175-letiyu so dnya rojdeniya A. S. Griboedoa," *Literaturnaya Armeniya* 1 (January 1970): 81–85.
25. There are plenty of influential courtier related with this family. I am preparing an article on this interesting family which will be developed into a book project, "A Family Called Language Box."
26. Unable to speak Turkish, the father spoke with his son in Circassian. His father behaved very arrogantly, and acquired his bad reputation. Abu l-Ma□āsin Ibn Taghrī Birdī, *History of Egypt, 1382–1469 A.D.*, tr. William Popper (Berkeley: University of California Press, 1957–63), 1–5.

27. Prince Temryuk of this family became father-in-law to Ivan IV. He claimed that he was a great grandson of Sultan Inal. This family produced many famous Russian generals after their conversion. Pavel Dmitrievich Dolgorukov, *Rossiiskaya rodoslovnaya kniga* (St. Petersburg: Tip. III Otdeleniya Sob. E.I.V. Kantselyarii, 1855), 2:36; E. H. Kusheva, *Narody Severnogo Kavkaza i ikh svyazi s Rossiei: vtoraya polovina XVI-30-e gody XVII veka* (Moskva: Izd-vo Akademii nauk SSSR, 1963), 109.
28. Jane Hathaway and Karl Barbir, *The Arab Lands under Ottoman Rule: 1516–1800* (New York: Pearson Longman, 2008), 96.
29. On the general accounts of their lives, see the articles in *Encyclopaedia of Islam*, new edition, vol. II, 184 (Davud Pasha) and vol. III, 992 (Ibrahim Begy). Janelidze and Silagadze's publications revealed their relations with the homeland. Davit Janelidze and Beniamin Silagadze, *K'art'veli mamluk'ebi egviatesa da eraqshi*, (Tbilisi: Sabchota Sakartvelo, 1967); and Beniamin Silagadze, *Eraqi mamluk't'a gamgeblobis kha 'nashi*, (Tbilisi: Metsniereba, 1978). Crecelius and Djaparidze's English article (see note 30) vividly illustrates the lives of the Georgian Mamluks, too.
30. Daniel Crecelius and Gotcha Djaparidze, "Relations of the Georgian Mamluks of Egypt with Their Homeland in the Last Decades of the Eighteenth Century," *Journal of the Economic and Social History of the Orient* 45, no. 3 (2002): 320–41; and Crecelius and Djaparidze, "Georgians in the Military Establishment in Egypt in the Seventeenth and Eighteenth Centuries," *Annales islamologique* 42 (2008): 313–39.
31. Crecelius and Djaparidze "Relations of the Georgian Mamluks," 331–39; Crecelius and Djaparidze, On Ibrahim's Georgian "household," see Crecelius and Djaparidze, "Georgians in the Military Establishment," 328.
32. Crecelius and Djaparidze, "Relations of the Georgian Mamluks," 328.
33. Crecelius and Djaparidze, "Relations of the Georgian Mamluks," 335-36.
34. Dolidze, I. ed., *Kartuli Samartlis Dzeglebi*, vol. 7, *Sasamartlo arza-okmebi* (Tbilisi: Metsniereba, 1981), 690–91.
35. Most of the personal names of this part are transliterated from Georgian article by Arjevanidze noted below.
36. Ivane Arjevanidze, "Ioseb Tsilosnis (Ali-Amedi-Efendis) sabiograpio masala," *Masalebi Sakartvelosa da Kavkasiis istoriisatvis* 1946, part I: 21–95. This article, written just after World War II, shed light on the interesting fate of "the last Mamluk" who returned to his homeland. This article consists of two sections. The second (which starts on p. 49, thus consisting of two thirds of the entire article) is an edition of collected materials, including many photos of the family. Part of the article was written in Russian, and part in French with Georgian translation.
37. Of course, Tsilosani's "return" to Russia and his subsequent fate was possibly influenced by the international circumstances of the time, that is, the rise of the Eastern Question. In 1831, Muhammad Ali challenged militarily his sovereign in his demand for the control of Greater Syria. Russia then became the protector of the interests of the Ottoman central court. In the Treaty of Hünkâr İskelesi (1833), Russia obtained the right to have the Ottomans close the Dardanelles to foreign warships, except those of Russia and the Ottoman Empire. In 1839 Tsilosani sent a letter stating that a new war had broken out between Egypt and the Ottoman court. This time, France backed Egypt, England, Austria, Prussia, and Russia backed the Ottomans. In 1840, the Treaty of London was concluded. Great Britain succeeded in changing the situation of the Dard-

anelles, which would now be closed to all military ships. Virginia H. Aksan, *Ottoman Wars, 1700–1870: An Empire Besieged* (Harlow, England: Pearson-Longman, 2007), 375, 407.
38. According to Arjevanidze, Tsilosani was well connected with intellectual circles in Tbilisi and St. Petersburg. Arjevanidze, "Ioseb Tsilosnis (Ali-Amedi-Efendis) sabiograpio masala," 42.
39. Interestingly Tsilosani held the rank of colonel (polkovnik) one year before his death in 1873. Abrama Enikolopian, who represented the interests of the Enikolopian family in Tbilisi around same period, also held the rank of colonel but seemingly much earlier in his age. Abrama was a grandson of his namesake Abrama (Abraham, Ibrahim), younger brother of Rostom Enikolopian, and an important interpreter after the Russian conquest of Georgia as mentioned earlier.

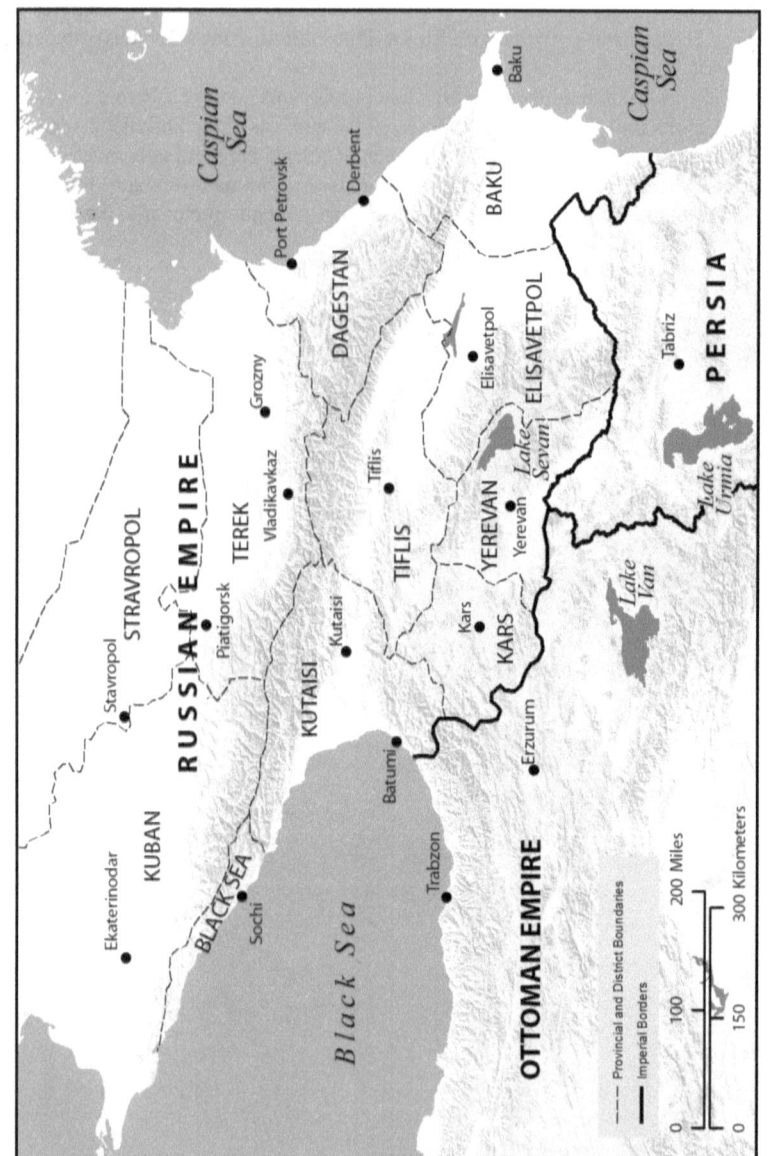

The Caucasus in 1903

Effects of Empire: Tsarism as Enabler and Constraint on the Peoples of Caucasia

RONALD GRIGOR SUNY

Among the various kinds of political communities and units that have existed historically, empires have been among the most ubiquitous, in many ways the precursors of the modern bureaucratic state. Anthony Pagden has traced the various meanings attached to empire in European discourses. In its original meaning in classical times *imperium* described the executive authority of Roman magistrates and eventually came to refer to "non-subordinate power." Such a usage can be found in the first line of Machiavelli's *The Prince*: "All the states and dominions which have had and have empire over men . . ."[1] By the sixteenth century, empire took on the meaning of *status*, state, the political relationships that held groups of people together in an extended system, but from Roman times on it already possessed one of the modern senses of empire as an immense state, an "extended territorial dominion."[2] Finally, "to claim to be an *imperator* [from Augustus' time] was to claim a degree, and eventually a kind of power, denied to mere kings."[3] Absolute or autocratic rule was then identified with empire, along with the idea that an empire referred to "a diversity of territories under a single authority."[4] Pagden emphasizes the durability of these discursive traditions. "All these three senses of the term *imperium*—as limited and independent or 'perfect' rule, as a territory embracing more than one political community, and as the absolute sovereignty of a single individual—

survive into the late eighteenth century and sometimes well beyond. All three derived from the discursive practices of the Roman empire, and to a lesser extent the Athenian and Macedonian empires."[5] Moreover, empire was connected with "the notion of a single exclusive world domain," both in Roman times and later, and the great European overseas empires, especially that of Spain, never quite abandoned "this legacy of universalism, developed over centuries and reinforced by a powerfully articulate learned elite."[6]

Though sensitive to the variety of historical meanings attached to empire, social scientists have attempted a more limited understanding of empire as a political relationship. Michael W. Doyle's definition—"Empire... is a relationship, formal or informal, in which one state controls the effective political sovereignty of another political society"—is extremely useful, even though he is concerned almost exclusively with non-contiguous empires.[7] Elaborating further he argues that empire is "a system of interaction between two political entities, one of which, the dominant metropole, exerts political control over the internal and external policy—the effective sovereignty—of the other, the subordinate periphery."[8] John A. Armstrong, as well, speaks of empire as "a compound polity that has incorporated lesser ones."[9] For my purposes, looking at contiguous empire-states that do not necessarily have states within them, political society must be defined more loosely than as state.[10]

Borrowing from Armstrong and Doyle, I define empire as a particular form of domination or control, between two units set apart in a hierarchical, inequitable relationship, more precisely a composite state in which a metropole dominates a periphery to the disadvantage of the periphery. Rather than limit empires and imperialism (the building and maintaining of empires) to relations between polities, I extend the definition of imperialism to the deliberate act or policy that furthers a state's extension or maintenance for the purpose of aggrandizement of that kind of direct or indirect political or economic control over any other inhabited territory which involves the inequitable treatment of those inhabitants in comparison with its own citizens or subjects. Like Doyle I emphasize that an imperial state differs from the broader category of multinational states, confederations, or federations in that it "is not organized on the basis of political equality among societies or individuals. The domain of empire is a people subject to unequal rule."[11] Not all multinational, multicultural, or multireligious states are necessarily empires, but where distinctions remain and treatment is unequal, as in areas that remain ethnically distinct, then the relationship continues to be imperial. Inequitable treatment might involve forms of cultural or linguistic discrimination or disadvantageous redistributive practices from the periphery to the metropole (but not necessarily, as, for example, in the Soviet empire). This ideal type of empire, then, is fundamentally different from the ideal type of the nation-state. While empire is inequitable rule over something different, nation-state rule is, at least in theory if not always in practice, the same for all members of the nation. Citizens of the nation have a different relationship with their state than do the subjects of empire.

Besides inequality and subordination, the relationship of the metropole to the periphery is marked by difference—by ethnicity, geographic separation, administrative distinction.[12] If peripheries are fully integrated into the metropole, as various appanage principalities were into Muscovy, and treated as well or badly as the metropolitan provinces, then the relationship is not imperial. Very importantly, the metropole need not be defined ethnically or geographically. It is the ruling institution. In several empires, rather than a geographic or ethnic distinction from the periphery, the ruling institution had a status or class character, a specially endowed nobility or political class, like the Osmanli in the Ottoman Empire, or the imperial family and upper layers of the landed gentry and bureaucracy in the Russian Empire, or, analogously, the Communist *nomenklatura* in the Soviet Union. In my understanding, neither tsarist Russia nor the Soviet Union was an ethnically "Russian Empire" with the metropole completely identified with a ruling Russian nationality. Rather, the ruling institution—nobility in one case, the Communist Party elite in the other—was multinational, though primarily Russian *and* ruled imperially over Russian and non-Russian subjects alike. In empire, unlike nations, the distance and difference of the rulers from the ruled was part of the ideological justification for the superordination of the ruling institution. The right to rule an empire resides with the ruling institution, not in the consent of the governed.

All states have centers, capital cities and central elites, which in some ways are superior to the other parts of the state, but in empires the metropole is uniquely sovereign, able to override routinely the desires and deci-

Echmiadzin Cathedral

sions of peripheral units.[13] The flow of goods, information, and power runs from periphery to metropole and back to periphery but seldom from periphery to periphery. The degree of dependence of periphery on metropole is far greater and more encompassing than in other kinds of states. Roads and railroads run to the capital; elaborate architectural and monumental displays mark the imperial center off from other centers; and the central imperial elite distinguishes itself in a variety of ways from both peripheral elites, often their servants and agents, and the ruled population.[14] The metropole benefits from the periphery in an inequitable way; there is "exploitation," at least there is the perception of such exploitation. That, indeed, is the essence of what being colonized means.

While subordination, inequitable treatment, and exploitation might be measured in a variety of ways, they are always inflected subjectively and normatively. As Beissinger has suggested:

> Any attempt to define empire in 'objective' terms—as a system of stratification, as a policy based on force, as a system of exploitation—fails in the end to capture what is undoubtedly the most important dimension of any imperial situation: perception. . . . Empires and states are set apart not primarily by exploitation, nor even by the use of force, but essentially by whether politics and policies are accepted as 'ours' or are rejected as 'theirs'.[15]

To this should be added that the perception of empire is not only about the attitude of peripheries but of metropoles as well. Empire exists even if peripheral populations are convinced that the result of their association with the empire is beneficial rather than exploitative, as long as the two conditions of distinction and subordination obtain. Indeed, much of the "post-colonialism" literature has dealt precisely with the ways in which hegemonic cultures of difference and development have sanctioned imperial relations and mediated resistance.

To sum up, empire is a composite state structure in which the metropole is distinct in some way from the periphery and the relationship between the two is conceived or perceived by metropolitan or peripheral actors as one of justifiable or unjustifiable inequity, subordination, and/or exploitation. "Empire" is not merely a form of polity but also a value-laden appellation that as late as the nineteenth century (and even in some usages well into our own) was thought of as the sublime form of political existence (think of New York as the "empire state") but which in the late twentieth century casts doubts about the legitimacy of a polity and even predicts its eventual, indeed inevitable, demise.[16] Thus, the Soviet Union, which a quarter of a century ago would have been described by most social scientists as a state and only occasionally, and usually by expressly/avowedly anti-Soviet analysts, as an empire, is almost universally described after its demise as an empire, since it now appears to have been an illegitimate, composite polity unable to contain the rising nations within it.

Following the lead of recent theorists of the nation, I define a nation as a group of people who imagines itself to be a political community that is distinct from the rest of humankind, believes that it shares characteristics, perhaps origins, values, historical experiences, language, territory, or any of many other elements, and on the basis of their defined culture deserves self-determination, which usually entails control of its own territory (the "homeland") and a state of its own.[17] Neither natural nor primordial but the result of hard constitutive intellectual and political work of elites and masses, nations exist in particular understandings of history, stories in which the nation is seen as the subject moving continuously through time, coming to self-awareness over many centuries.[18] Though there may be examples of political communities in the distant past that approach our notions of modern nations, in the modern era political communities exist within a discourse that came together in the late eighteenth and early nineteenth centuries around the notion of bounded territorial sovereignties in which the "people" constituted as a nation provide the legitimacy to the political order. From roughly the late eighteenth century to the present the state merged with the "nation," and almost all modern states claimed to be nation-states, either in an ethnic or civic sense, with governments deriving power from and exercising it in the interest of the nation. Modern states legitimized themselves in reference to the nation and the claims to popular sovereignty implicit in the discourse of the nation.[19]

Though the discourse of the nation began as an expression of state patriotism, through the nineteenth century it increasingly became ethnicized until the "national community" was understood to be a cultural community of shared language, religion, and/or other characteristics with a durable, antique past, shared kinship, common origins, and narratives of progress through time. Lost to time were the ways in which notions of shared pasts and common origins were constructed and reimagined, how primary languages themselves were selected from dialects and elevated to dominance through print and schooling, and how history itself was employed to justify claims to the world's real estate. Nationalists strove to make the nation and the state congruent, an almost utopian goal, and it is not a great stretch to argue that much of modern history has been about making nations and states fit together in a world where the two almost never match.

By the twentieth century such imagined communities were the most legitimate basis for the constitution of states, displacing dynastic, religious, and class discourses—and coincidentally challenging alternative formulas for legitimation, like those underpinning empires. Once-viable imperial states became increasingly vulnerable to nationalist movements that in turn gained strength from the new understanding that states ought to represent, if not coincide, with nations. The simultaneous rise of notions of democratic representation of subaltern interests accentuated the fundamental tension between inequitable imperial relationships and horizontal conceptions of national citizenship. Though liberal states with representative institutions, styling themselves as democracies, could be (and were) effective imperial powers in the overseas empires of Great Britain, France, Belgium, and the Netherlands, the great contiguous empires resisted democratization that would have undermined the right to rule of the dominant imperial elite and the very hierarchical and inequitable relationship between metropole and periphery in the empire. While empires were among the most ubiquitous and long-lived polities in premodern history, they were progressively subverted in modern times by the powerful combination of nationalism and democracy.[20]

Modernizing Empires

Modern empires, like tsarist Russia in the nineteenth century, were caught between maintaining the privileges and distinctions that kept the traditional elites in power or considering reforms along liberal lines that would have undermined the old ruling classes. While the great "bourgeois" overseas empires of the nineteenth century were able to liberalize, even democratize in the metropoles, at the same time maintaining harsh repressive regimes in the colonies, pursuing different policies in core and periphery was far more difficult in contiguous empires than in non-contiguous ones. While it was possible to have a democratic metropole and colonized peripheries in overseas empires, as the examples of Britain, France, and Belgium show, it was potentially destabilizing to have constitutionalism or liberal democracy in only part of a contiguous empire. In Russia the privileges enjoyed by the Grand Duchy of Finland, or even the constitution granted to Bulgaria, an independent state outside the empire, were constant reminders to the tsar's educated subjects of his refusal to allow them similar institutions. Here is a major tension of contiguous empires. Some kind of separation, apartheid, is essential to maintain a democratic and non-democratic political order in a single state. But this is a highly unstable compromise as the governments of South Africa and Israel discovered in the twentieth century.

In contiguous empires, where the distinction between the nation and the empire is more easily muddled than in overseas empires, ruling elites may attempt to construct hybrid notions of an empire-nation, as in tsarist Russia or the Ottoman Empire in the nineteenth century.[21] Responding to the challenges presented by the efficiencies of the new national states, imperial elites promoted a transition from "ancien regime" empires to "modern" empires, from a more polycentric and differentiated polity in which regions maintained quite different legal, economic, and even political structures, to a more centralized, bureaucratized state in which state elites homogenized laws, economic practices, and even customs and dialects,. The more modern empires adopted a number of strategies to restabilize their rule. In Russia the monarchy became more "national" in its self-image and public representation, drawing it closer to the people it ruled. In Austro-Hungary the central state devolved power to several of the non-ruling peoples, moving the empire toward becoming a more egalitarian multinational state. In the Ottoman Empire modernizing bureaucrats abandoned certain traditional hierarchical practices that privileged Muslims over non-Muslims, and in the reforming era known as Tanzimat they attempted to create a civic nation of all peoples of the empire, an Ottomanist idea of a new imperial community. In the last two decades of the nineteenth century the tsarist government attempted yet another strategy, a policy of administrative and cultural Russification that privileged a single nationality. The Young Turks after 1908 flirted with everything from an Ottomanist liberalism to Pan-Islamic, and increasingly nationalist reconfigurations of their empire.[22] But modernizing imperialists were caught between these new projects of homogenization and rationalization, and policies and structures that maintained distance and difference from their subjects as well as differentiations and disadvantages among the peoples of the empire. Modernizing empires searched for new legitimation formulas that softened rhetorics of conquest and divine sanction and emphasized the civilizing mission of the imperial metropole, its essential competence in a new project of development.

Given the unevenness of the economic transformations of the nineteenth and twentieth centuries, all within a highly competitive international environment, most states, even quite conservative imperial states like the Ottoman and Romanov empires, undertook state programs of economic and social "modernization." Developmentalism was soon deeply embedded both in national and imperial state policies. Needing to justify the rule of foreigners over peoples who were constituting themselves as nations, the idea of developing inferior or uncivilized peoples became a dominant source of imperial legitimation and continued well into the twentieth century.[23]

There is a subversive dialectic in developmentalism, however. Its successes create the conditions for imperial failure. If the developmentalist program succeeds among the colonized people, realizing material well-being and intellectual sophistication, urbanism and industrialism, social mobility and knowledge of the world, the justification for foreign imperial rule over a "backward" people evaporates. Indeed, rather than suppressing nation-making and nationalism, imperialism far more often provides conditions and stimulation for the construction of new nations. Populations are ethnographically described, statistically enumerated, ascribed characteristics and functions, and reconceive themselves in ways that qualify them as "nations." Not accidentally the map of the world at the end of the twentieth century is marked by dozens of states with boundaries drawn by imperialism. And if clearly defined and articulated nations do not exist within these states by the moment of independence, then state elites busily set about creating national political communities to fill out the fledgling state.

Developmentalism, of course, was not the project of "bourgeois" nation-states and empires alone, but of self-styled socialist ones as well. The problem grew when empires, which justified their rule as agents of modernity and modernization, as instruments of development and progress, achieved their stated task too well, supplied their subordinated populations with languages of aspiration and resistance (as Cooper and Packard put it, "What at one level appears like a discourse of control is at another a discourse of entitlement."[24]), and indeed created subjects that no longer required empire in the way the colonizers claimed. This dialectical reversal of the justification for empire, embedded in the theory and practice of modernization, was, in my view, also at the very core of the progressive decay of the Soviet Empire. In a real sense the Communist Party effectively made itself irrelevant. Who needed a "vanguard" when you now had an urban, educated, mobile, self-motivated society? Who needed imperial control from Moscow when national elites and their constituents were able to articulate their own interests in terms sanctioned by Marxism-Leninism in the idea of national self-determination?

The Empire of the Tsars

Russia followed a particular logic of empire-building. After acquiring territory, usually by conquest, often by expanding settlement, the agents of the tsar co-opted local elites into the service of the empire.[25] But in many peripheries, like the Volga, Siberia, Transcaucasia, and Central Asia, integration stopped with the elites (and only partially) and did not include the basic peasant or nomadic populations which retained their tribal, ethnic, and religious identities. Some elites, like the Tatar and Ukrainian nobles, dissolved into the Russian *dvoriantsvo*, but others, like the German barons of the Baltic or the Swedish aristocrats of Finland, retained privileges and separate identities. "Nationalizing," homogenizing policies, integrating disparate peoples into a common "Russian" community (particularly among the nobles) coexisted with policies of discrimination and distinction. After subduing their khanate, Russia gave the Bashkirs rights as a military host in the Volga region. Some peoples, like the Georgians, were allowed to keep their customary laws; German barons, Greek and Armenian merchants enjoyed economic and legal benefits, while Jews were restricted from migrating out of the Pale of Settlement. The religious and social life of Muslims was regulated by the state.

Religion remained the principal marker of difference between Russians and non-Russians, and religious identity was believed to reveal essential qualities that helped to predict behavior. Orthodox Christians were expected to be more loyal than the duplicitous Muslims. Not infrequently, "enlightened" state officials argued that conversion to Orthodox Christianity would strengthen the empire as well as bring civilization to the benighted populations of the borderlands.[26] Though efforts at such religious "Russification" were haphazard, they reinforced the perceptual connection between Russianness and Orthodoxy. Beginning with Peter's efforts to modernize Russia, the state and church intensified the previously sporadic attempts to bring the benefits of Orthodoxy and western learning to the benighted non-Russians of the east and south.[27]

As Europe went through the fallout from 1789, Russia represented "the most imperial of nations, comprising more peoples than any other. The academician Heinrich Storch boasted of the ethnographic variety of Russia in 1797, commenting that 'no other state on earth contains such a variety of inhabitants.'"[28] In its own imagery Russia was the Roman Empire reborn. As the discourse of the nation took shape in and after the French Revolution and the Napoleonic wars, as concepts of "the people" and popular sovereignty spread through Europe, the traditional monarchical concepts of the foreign tsar held at bay any concession to the new national populism. Russian resistance to Napoleon, as well as the expansion of the empire into the Caucasus and Finland, only accentuated the imperial image of irresistible power, displayed physically on both battlefield and parade ground by the martinet tsars of the early nineteenth century.[29]

Russia emerged from the Napoleonic wars even more imperial than it had been in the eighteenth century. Now the possessor of the Grand Duchy of Finland, the emperor served there as a constitutional monarch and was to observe the public law of the Grand Duchy, and in the Kingdom of Poland (1815–32), he served as Tsar' Polskii, the constitutional king of Poland. According to the Fundamental Laws codified in 1832, "the

Emperor of Russia is an autocratic (*samoderzhavnyi*) and unlimited (*neogranichennyi*) monarch," but his realm was governed by laws, a *Rechtsstaat*, and was distinct from the despotisms of the East.[30] The tsar stood apart and above his people; his people remained diverse not only ethnically but in terms of the institutions through which they were ruled. Victorious Russia, the conservative bulwark against the principles of the French Revolution, was in many ways the antithesis of nationalism. Alexander I expressed this personally in his scheme for a Holy Alliance in which various states would consider themselves members "of a single Christian nation" ruled over by the "Autocrat of the Christian People," Jesus Christ.[31]

The "modernizing" practices of eighteenth- and nineteenth-century Russian emperors and bureaucrats that homogenized disparate economic and legal practices were certainly significant, but they must be placed against programs and policies that moved in another direction, creating new or reinforcing old differences, distinctions, privileges, and disadvantages based on social class, region, ethnicity, or religion. Among Russians the literary elite developed a sense of national distinction in the eighteenth century, but through the first half of the next century there was very little sense of nation in the developing Western conception of a political community in which the people were the source of legitimacy and even sovereignty. Russia was a state and an empire in which its population was divided horizontally among dozens of ethnicities and religions and vertically between ruling and privileged estates and the great mass of the peasant population. These divisions were formalized in the law and fixed most people and peoples in positions of discrimination and disadvantage. Such hierarchies and separations inhibited the development of the kinds of horizontal bonds of fraternity and solidarity that already marked the rhetoric of the nation in the West. To the very last days of the empire the Romanov regime remained imperial in this sense, a complex, differentiated, hierarchical, traditional ancient regime, with structures and laws that restricted efforts at equalization and homogenization. The horizontal, fraternal ties that ideally mark citizenship in the nation-form could not be established in a system so embedded in hierarchy and distinction, disdain and distance from the great mass of the population.

Oil gusher outside Baku

The Empire Comes to the Caucasus

Caucasia was the borderland where the Muslim world of the Ottoman Empire and Persia met Christian Armenia and Georgia. With the coming of the Russians in the first decades of the nineteenth century, the peoples of the Caucasus witnessed the most profound transformation of their society since the coming of Christianity in the fifth century. Armenians gained a new level of security, and their upper and middle classes developed as entrepreneurs in the towns. United for the first time in nearly five hundred years by the Russian Empire, Georgians began a gradual social metamorphosis that ended their rural isolation, eroded the power of the traditional landed nobility, and created an urban Georgian population for the first time in their history. Georgians were still largely a rural people; for example, ninety-five percent of Gori district's inhabitants were peasants. The legal emancipation of landlord serfs was completed in the 1870s, and noble landlords reluctantly and slowly granted permission for peasants to move freely from their villages. Peasants who lost their land or their jobs as household servants or had their plots reduced were compelled to find new work in the towns. The first factories deserving of that name were opened in the largest city of Georgia, Tiflis (Tbilisi), and to the east in the multinational oil-producing center, Baku. In 1860 an Englishman named Rooks opened the first "mechanized workshop," and five years later the Armenian Mirzoev established the first textile mill in Tiflis. "Tatars," as they were called at the time, moved into the oil districts, joined by immigrants from Persia.

From the beginning of the nineteenth century, when the Russian Empire annexed the Georgian kingdoms and principalities, European culture steadily filtered into the towns of south Caucasia, starting from the top down with the urban aristocracy and the commercial middle class. Already by the 1840s Georgian and Armenian townswomen in Tiflis were either modifying their dress along European lines or adopting completely the latest fashions from Paris. The newer districts of the city were built, not in the traditional Georgian styles, but according to the dictates of neo-classicism. "It is not to be forgotten," wrote the traveler A. L. Zisserman, "that [comparing] Tiflis in 1842 and 1878 is [like] Asia and Europe; now one has to search for oriental peculiarities, but then they simply hit you in the eye."[32] Gori, however, enjoyed a slower pace of life, without the variety of a city or the attractions of a lively nightlife. One of the few entertainments for the young boys of the town was the occasional visit of the old *mestvire* (troubadour), Sandro, whom they followed through the streets, forgetting the enmities of the different neighborhoods, enraptured by his ballads of the bandits Arsen and Tato and the seventeenth-century rebel against the Persians, the noble Georgi Saakadze.[33] What news of Georgia or the outside world there was came either from the local barbers or the few copies of the Georgian-language journal *tsnobis purtseli* (Newssheet) that circulated from hand to hand.[34] As Caucasian styles, heavily indebted to the long years of Persian and Turkish dominion, retreated before Russian and European customs and practices, urban life grew more distinct from village life, which remained bound to older local traditions.

Along with customs and material life, identities shifted among the Caucasian peoples. Georgia's religion, intertwined as it was with ethnic culture and patriotism, came under serious challenge by the tsarist authorities, who by the last quarter of the nineteenth century grew increasingly suspicious of national expressions. The Georgian Orthodox Church, which might have been a vehicle for the preservation and promotion of Georgian, was hobbled by its doctrinal and institutional subordination to the Holy Synod of the Russian Orthodox Church. In 1811 it had lost its autocephaly, and the last catholicos (head of the church) was removed, sent into exile, and replaced by an exarch appointed by the tsar. By the last decades of the century Georgian bishops were sent elsewhere to serve, and Georgia's ecclesiastical hierarchy was largely Russian.[35] Church authorities suppressed Georgian religious practices and the use of the vernacular in the service and in teaching. As the church lost its position as defender of the Georgians, the nascent Georgian intelligentsia, largely made up of provincial noblemen, displaced the religious elite as the principal definer of Georgian culture. In the absence of a Georgian state the intellectuals became the inventors and carriers of what they determined to be the recovered national traditions. As the architects of a new nationalist discourse, they disseminated ideas that held sway among the elite until challenged at the turn of the century by a particularly Georgian Marxism.

Armenians were a favored people in the early nineteenth century, envisioned by Russians as valuable entrepreneurs. Their church was given a charter in 1836 guaranteeing it a degree of independence but ultimate subordination to the power of the tsarist state. But toward the end of the century the rise of nationalism and the revolutionary movement enticed young Armenians, who formed small revolutionary circles and eventually political parties. Although their revolutionary activity was aimed primarily at liberating their ethnic compatriots across the border in the Ottoman Empire, Armenian activists came to be viewed as dangerous subversive elements by tsarist authorities. In a climate where ethnic stereotypes were the discursive currency of the day, Russian officials branded Armenians more generally with the accusation that they were a threat to the empire. In 1903 the government of Nicholas II appropriated the properties of the Armenian Church, unilaterally abrogating the Polozhenie of 1836. The Armenian Revolutionary Federation (Dashnaktsutiun) organized resistance, and the last years of the tsarist regime were marked by tensions between the state and its Armenian subjects.

The Muslims of the Caucasus were generally treated as second- or even third-class subjects. They were referred to by Russians as *temnye* (dark or uncivilized). Their rights were restricted, and a general condescension by Christians was evident. Yet some Muslims in Baku managed to enrich themselves in the oil business, publish newspapers and journals, and patronize a small Muslim intelligentsia. The identity of most Muslims remained religious and local, but by the second decade of the twentieth century some activists had begun tentatively to articulate an idea of an Azerbaijani nation.[36]

The clash of cultures, Russian and Caucasian, is central to the nationalist and imperial narratives of the nineteenth century. In the story told by nationalists, an ancient people with a deeply embedded ethnoreligious culture confronts an emasculating imperial power determined to annihilate that culture and people through repression and assimilation. Opposed to that story, and ultimately far less influential, was the imperial story told by Russian officialdom and its supporters of a great state, tolerant and caring of its constituent peoples, that faces ungrateful and rebellious subjects subversive both to the civilizing mission of the empire and a benevolent state. Here repression, as with other imperial projects, is justified in the name of order and progress.

Both stories are founded on clear lines of difference between ethnic cultures, on the one hand, and between empire and nation, on the other. What is largely lost in these narratives is the constitutive effects of imperial rule on the making of nations within the empire as well as the ways in which peoples shared, borrowed, and migrated between different cultures. Instead of static, fully formed, and clearly bounded cultures confronting each other, nineteenth-century Russians and Caucasian peoples were simultaneously evolving, changing, and in many ways affecting each other. Georgian and Armenian, as well as other non-Russian, intellectuals spoke of the recovery of a primordial nationhood that the empire was determined to suppress. Ironically, however, the empire, with its face turned toward Europe, aided the very process of nation-making by fostering education, social mobility, and the means of communication (railroads, roads, and telegraphs) by which isolated, illiterate villagers grew to imagine they were part of a larger community, the nation.[37] The growth of cities, as well as the peace and security enforced by the imperial state, cultivated the ground from which nationalist intellectuals grew to become the most forceful voices of the nation. Modernity was associated with Russia, tradition with Georgia or Armenian, and in small towns and villages a certain suspicion of the novel and unfamiliar reigned. This is illustrated by a story told by a boyhood friend of Iosip Jughashvili, the future Stalin. When his little pal, Soso Davrishevi, returned from a sojourn with his cultivated Armenian relatives in Tiflis, outfitted in a European-style sailor suit, complete with red pompom on his hat, his Gori companions were both fascinated and appalled by his attire. Soso Jughashvili grabbed his hat roughly, and before the little sailor's grandmother could rescue him, he lay on the ground nearly naked.[38]

The ambivalent relationship of Caucasians to the Russian empire is illustrated by the Georgian case. Georgia's relationship with Russia was ambiguous and could be read in very different ways. Kings of Georgia from the fifteenth century on had sent embassies to the Russian court requesting aid and security from the Ottoman and Persian incursions that repeatedly threatened the Caucasian Christians. At a moment when Georgia's very existence hung in the balance, at the end of the eighteenth century, the long reigning King of Kartli-Kakheti (Eastern Georgia), Erekle II (1762–98), petitioned Catherine the Great for assistance against the Persians, and in 1783 he signed the Treaty of Giorgievsk that placed his kingdom under Russian protection. But just before Georgia suffered the ravages of Shah Agha Mohammed's armies in 1795, the Empress withdrew the Russian troops beyond the high Caucasus The Russians soon pushed the Persians out of the South Caucasus and proceeded to break their own agreement with the last Georgian king, Giorgi XII (1798–1800), fully annexing his kingdom in 1801. Soon all of the Georgian principalities were governed as Russian provinces, along with regions inhabited by Armenians and Caucasian Muslims.

The imposition of Russian law, including serfdom, tsarist bureaucratic absolutism, and a cultural condescension toward local customs and practices stirred resentment and opposition among segments of the nobility and the peasants.[39] On the one hand, the need for Russian protection and the hope for a northern route to European enlightenment inspired dedication, even affection, for the tsarist empire among many Georgians. But, on the other, Russia was a brutal master and its culture a debased version of Europe's. The highpoint of Georgian Russophilia was reached during the administration of Viceroy Mikhail Vorontsov (1845–54) and Prince Aleksandr Bariatinskii (1856–62) when many Georgian nobles loyally served the tsar in government and the army, and the first intellectuals (known as the *tergdaleulni*, drinkers of the waters of the Terek, the river that separated Russia land from Georgia) made their way to Petersburg and Moscow to acquire European learning. When they returned to their homeland, however, making their way down the Georgian Military Highway, through the Darial Pass along the Terek, these gentry intellectuals thought of themselves as *mamulishvilebi* (sons of the fatherland) with a new appreciation of what was most valuable in their own people.

At first, as Georgian national awareness spread from a narrow circle of writers to the broader readership of their newspapers and novels, the relationship between Georgian intellectuals and Russians remained symbiotic rather than conflictual. Stimulated by European and Russian ethnographic and philological studies, interest and pride in the Georgian language grew along with a new appreciation of folk music, Georgia's history, and ethnography.[40] By the 1870s, however, the vulnerability of Georgian culture before the twin threats of the Russian language and the attractions of a more Europeanized urban life convinced several Georgian journalists and teachers to promote the teaching of their own language. In 1879 a number of Georgian cultural nationalists formed the Society to Spread Literacy among Georgians in Tiflis and began to publish textbooks and grammars.[41]

The rediscovery of Georgianness was largely the project of Russian-educated Georgian intellectuals and political activists—the poets Rapiel Eristavi, Ilia Chavchavadze, and Akaki Tsereteli; the journalists Sergei Meskhi and Niko Nikoladze; and eventually the Georgian Marxists—as well as dozens of other lesser-known school teachers, librarians, booksellers, grammarians, and chorus directors. At the center of the national effort was a new respect for the Georgian language and the promotion of its literary culture. Within the literary tradition that extended from medieval hymnographers through secular poets, three works stood as the principal pillars of Georgian literature—the Bible; Shota Rustaveli's epic poem of the twelfth century, *vepkhistqaosani* (The Knight in the Panther's Skin); and *kartlis_tskhovreba* (The Life of Georgia), the chronicles that collectively recorded the history of the Georgian monarchies. Committed to reviving the Georgian language and literature and preserving what they took to be the essence of their culture, poets, scholars, and journalists selected from the chaotic past of traditions and symbols to inspire a new sense of nationhood. Unlike many peoples of the Russian Empire, Georgians were privileged to have a history of statehood, a recoverable record of heroic battles preserved in the royal chronicles, and glorious periods of art and architecture physically present on the landscape. Consonant with the developing national consciousness of other peoples, the *tergdaleulni* articulated a notion of nation based on the ethnic culture of the people, rather than primarily on religion, and emphasized harmony between nobles and peasants and development through education and economic growth.[42] The nobleman Ilia Chavchavadze (1837–1907), universally recognized as the most important nationalist writer and poet, urged Georgians to value their common culture. Rather than thinking of themselves as Imeretians, Gurians, Megrelians, or Kartvelians, or dismissing the peasants as uncultured, they should think as a coherent nation: "If Georgian is not their common name, then what is common to all of them? . . . if the people of the countryside are not Georgians, then who are they?"[43]

Along with Armenians, Ukrainians, Estonians, and other peoples of the tsarist empire, Georgians were thinking nationally at the moment when the imperial state hoped to create its own "imperial nation" of all the loyal subjects of the tsar. Imperial patriots, whose primary allegiances were to the emperor and his empire, could be found among all the peoples of the empire, including the Georgians. But the tsarist government grew fearful of non-Russian nationalisms, particularly after the Polish rebellion of 1863, and as it tried to contain expressions of the nation it only compounded the problem. Liberal Europe presented a model of the national future that inspired intellectuals of small nationalities to think beyond empire and autocracy. The modern world was associated with new notions of citizenship, constitutionalism, and popular representation. Multiethnic autocratic empires appeared to be archaic forms of political organization inappropriate for modern times. Even as they looked back to imagined golden ages and traditional ways of life, nationalist intellectuals associated modernity with the revival of the nation, the freeing of the ethnic essence, and the release of the repressed potential of the national culture. The great paradox of empire was that its civilizing mission created the very people whose education, mobility, and exposure to the West transformed them into opponents of empire. Many who had once been loyal servitors of the tsar earlier in the century turned into proponents of their nations, even as they attempted to conceive schemes for reconciling nation with empire short of full separation and statehood.

As Georgians came to the towns in the last decades of the nineteenth century, they found people of other religions and languages, Armenians and Russians primarily. Contact heightened awareness of the distinctions among peoples, but at the same time the boundaries between ethnicities were occasionally crossed, in school and through public activity. While difference did not necessarily imply hostility or conflict, great importance was given to ethnicity and religion, especially when ethnicity overlapped with class and differences in power. Very often Armenians occupied more privileged positions, as merchants or factory owners. In a provincial capital like Jughashvili's Gori the reach of Russian rule was limited. Yet the garrison stood as a reminder of tsarist power, and the execution of peasant rebels or "bandits" reinforced the impression that behind the tax collectors and local bureaucrats stood the army and the police.

For much of the first century of Russian rule, the tsarist state did not interfere decisively with the customs or even the customary law of the Georgians. Traditions were intact, though changing, as were kinship and friendship networks. The very choice to speak Georgian on the streets or in the markets excluded any Russians nearby. Through the year various religious holidays and popular festivals affirmed Georgians' preferred understanding of their history. The most important festival, the carnival of *qeenoba*, marked a long ago conquest of Georgia by the Persian shah and a victorious uprising of the Georgians. Such invasions and rebellions were so numerous in Georgian history that the revelers referred to no specific battle. In the various towns, two sides were formed, one symbolically representing the Persians, the other the Georgians. The shah's forces occupied the town until mid-day. Then the Georgian side came forth; fights broke out; and the shah was thrown into the river. In the evening a massive fistfight brought the festivities to an end.[44]

The wider expression of national consciousness among Georgians and other non-Russian peoples in the 1870s stimulated in turn a reaction among Russian officials, suspicious of the potential claims of the empire's non-Russians. State policy toward the national borderlands had usually aimed at the legal integration of the various peoples but had traditionally permitted local customs and languages a degree of autonomy. By the 1880s, however, the Emperor Alexander III (1881–94) turned toward a policy of cultural Russification directed toward expanding the use of Russian in educational and administrative institutions. Such a threat to an emerging national identity dramatically affected the Georgian intelligentsia.

Like much of the rest of the Russian Empire, Georgia experienced a revival in political activity in 1894. A new emperor, Nicholas II, ascended the throne, and liberal nobles pinned their hopes for broadening the range of expression in the country on the young monarch. Although the tsar's initial response was to call their petitions "senseless dreams," the long dormant oppositional elements in society—liberal gentry in local and provincial assemblies (*zemstva*), educated professionals, and a growing number of revolutionary intellectuals—now sought both legal and illegal means to expand their influence. In Georgia, language was one of the battlefields on which Georgians tested their loyalties to their two "homelands," Georgia and Russia. Knowing Georgian and therefore being able to speak to the people gave the first generation of Georgian national intellectuals, like Ilia Chavchavadze, a claim to leadership of the nation they were bringing into being. Their gentry nationalism asserted the value of Georgian language and culture and lauded the unity of all classes of the nation. Chavchavadze expressed hostility toward what he saw as destructive anti-national forces:

the disruption of the traditional harmony and unity of Georgian society by Russian officials and the rapacious capitalist intrusions of Armenian merchants and industrialists. By the time he published an uncensored version of his *Letters of a Traveler* (1892), first written some thirty years earlier, his idea of a Georgia without capitalism or class strife had become an impossible utopia.[45] The old man grew increasingly conservative and closer to tsarist autocracy, while younger Georgian intellectuals were already moving toward a different vision. Rather than simple preservation of traditional culture and social harmony, the young radicals proposed aligning their country with what appeared to be the movement of history, with the direction things were actually going.

A small group of young intellectuals, which included the former seminarians Noe Zhordania, Pilipe Makharadze, and Mikha Tskhakaia, had been meeting since December 1892 to organize a political "party" around a revolutionary program. Zhordania and Makharadze—the former to become the leader of the Georgian Mensheviks and the latter the leader of the Georgian Bolsheviks—had left the seminary with "wolves' tickets," certificates that prohibited them from entering a university. Compelled to enroll in the Veterinarian Institute in Warsaw, they imbibed the dual intoxications of Marxism and anti-tsarist nationalism of "Russian" Poland. Their Polish experience solidified their opposition to Russian autocracy, and the newly-minted Marxists returned home confident that European Social Democracy laid out Georgia's path to the modern world. Not themselves completely free of nationalist sentiments, the young radicals nevertheless distanced themselves from the gentry nationalists around Chavchavadze and self-consciously adopted the internationalist language of Marxism. Inspired by both the traditions of Russian revolutionary Populism as well as Marx, they sought a way out of the double oppression they believed afflicted Georgia—the burden of Russian absolutism and the growing power of Armenian and foreign capital.

Zhordania and his associates began collaborating with the journal *kvali* (Furrow), whose editor, the liberal Giorgi Tsereteli, soon dubbed them *mesame dasi* (the third group) and thus the historic successors to the "enlighteners" of the 1860s (*pirveli dasi*, first group) and the liberal reformers of the 1870s (*meore dasi*, second group). Tsereteli reported in *kvali* the provocative speech of the firebrand "Silva" Jibladze at the funeral of the socialist writer, Egnate Ingoroqva (Ninoshvili) (1859–94). "Our contemporary life," Jibladze proclaimed, "presents two opposing camps or classes. On one side are the representatives of physical and mental labor; on the other are the bourgeois-capitalist parasites."[46] For young Georgian intellectuals, the funeral oration was like a bell in the still of the night. Something dormant was coming alive.

Although the group's ideological profile remained vague and eclectic for some time to come, the polemic directed against Chavchavadze's newspaper, *iveria*, helped to clarify important distinctions.[47] In the summer of 1894 a major programmatic article by Zhordania was, after much debate, approved by the group's members and published in the legal journal *moambe* (Bulletin). Here several themes that would be associated with *mesame dasi* were explicitly expressed: a commitment to social progress in a westernizing direction (a challenge to Chavchavadze's nostalgia for agrarian, seigniorial Georgia), a willingness to work with other nationalities (as opposed to *iveria*'s passionate Armenophobia), and a reliance on the notion of class conflict both in their social analysis and their political strategy (in contrast to Chavchavadze's ideal of social harmony under noble patriarchy).[48] Zhordania elaborated his class interpretation of Georgia's history and announced that "our country has already imperceptively stood on the road of industry; the nation has already pushed its head into the capitalist vise."[49]

Zhordania's article, "Economic Development and Nationality," appeared within months of Soso Jughashvili's arrival in Tiflis and soon became a major topic of conversation, particularly among students and young intellectuals. They sensed an energetic new force had entered Georgian life, an *akhali taoba* (new generation), and its compelling analysis of Georgia's dual social and cultural humiliation converted many to the new thinking. Zhordania soon became the acknowledged leader of this new intellectual and political movement, and eventually the editor of *kvali*. But while his path and Soso's would cross at crucial moments over their long careers, the two men could not have been more different. Zhordania, the son of impoverished nobles from a small town in Guria, Western Georgia, was a tall, slim man with a black beard and the manners of an aristocrat.[50] Modest and speaking with a slight stutter, he reminded an acolyte of a village teacher. His influence and power came from his writings. Applying histor-

Tiflis

ical materialism to the history of Georgia's national formation, Zhordania argued that while "language is the first sign of nationality," only real material transformation linked the disparate regions of Georgia together and led to the consolidation of the nation. And just as economic development has created a new Georgia, so in the future the national and the social struggles had to be combined in order to win freedom for the nation.

Zhordania's Marxism demystified the nation and rendered it a product of social forces. He provided Georgians with an ostensibly supra-nationalist analysis that at one and the same time offered a means of overcoming the dual oppression of Russian autocracy and Armenian capital. His version of history placed Georgia on the same trajectory as the advanced capitalist countries of Western Europe and singled out the embryonic working class of the Russian Empire as the instrument that would bring down the whole apparatus of state and economic power. Zhordania laid out the path by which backward, exoticized Georgia reached Europe and became part of the most advanced and progressive social movement of the time. Most impressively for the younger generation like Soso and his friends, this analysis explained the very changes in the social life of their country that they were experiencing. Moreover, it linked them in a common cause with Russian revolutionaries. Young Russian Marxists—Petr Struve, Vladimir Lenin, Iulii Martov, Aleksandr Potresov, and others—continued and expanded the earlier onslaught of Georgii Plekhanov, the "father of Russian Marxism," on the peasant socialism of the Populists (*narodniki*). The latter's notion that Russia could avoid capitalism and remain a land of small peasant farming was contradicted by the rapid industrialization and urban growth that Russia was experiencing. The prognosis of the Marxists that Russia (and within it, Georgia) would repeat the experience of Europe and America—massive industry, urban concentration, the emergence of the proletariat—seemed daily to be confirmed.

At the same time *mesame dasi* confidently put forth its own claim to be the new leaders of the Georgian people. They easily overwhelmed their principal opponents, the pathetically poor and discouraged nobles. Georgians had neither a state of their own nor even an effective, politically potent dominant class. Unlike the Armenians in their midst, who could boast an entrepreneurial "bourgeoisie," Georgians were divided between a declining gentry and peasants suffering from the onslaughts of a market economy that drove many into the industrial suburbs of the towns. Marxists stepped into a political void, a vacuum of leadership that gave the small Georgian intelligentsia, itself emerging from déclassé nobles and the sons of priests and teachers (and even cobblers), a weight in society far greater than its numbers would suggest. Young *intelligenti* (committed intellectuals) became the definers of the national agenda in this moment of transition and cultural crisis.

The stories of the Armenians and Azerbaijanis differ in detail from the Georgian story—Armenian parties were more nationalist than socialist, and Azerbaijani parties developed only quite late and remained small until the revolution—but the histories of all three peoples are illustrative of the power of empire to foster the material and discursive conditions for the reimagining of identities along national lines. Increased social communication fostered by new markets, railroads, newspapers, and greater ease of travel allowed people to become more aware of ethnic compatriots and the distinctions between themselves and ethnic others. Russian education and example, as well as exposure to Europe and the Ottoman Empire, helped generate the ethnic intellectuals that articulated and spread the European-inspired discourses of the nation. Repression and attempts to create supranational loyalties to the dynastic empire of the Romanovs only accelerated the turn of peoples to identification with the national and socialist activists.

Notes

1. Anthony Pagden, *Lords of All the World: Ideologies of Empire in Spain, Britain, and France, c. 1500–c. 1800* (New Haven and London: Yale University Press, 1995), 12.
2. Ibid., 15.
3. Ibid.
4. Ibid., 16.
5. Ibid., 17.
6. Ibid., 27–28.
7. Michael W. Doyle, *Empires* (Ithaca: Cornell University Press, 1986), 45.
8. Ibid., 12.
9. John A. Armstrong, *Nations before Nationalism* (Chapel Hill: The University of North Carolina Press, 1982), 131.
10. Doyle, *Empires*, 45.
11. Ibid., 36.
12. As Alexander J. Motyl argues, the peripheries must be distinct by population—class, ethnicity, religion, or something else—have a distinct territory, and be either a distinct

polity or a distinct society. ["From Imperial Decay to Imperial Collapse: The Fall of the Soviet Empire in Comparative Perspective," in Richard L. Rudolph and David F. Good (eds.), *Nationalism and Empire: The Habsburg Empire and the Soviet Union* (New York: St. Martin's Press, 1992), 18].
13. Of course, as an imperial metropole grows weaker and peripheries stronger, as in the Habsburg Empire after 1848, it is forced to negotiate with powerful peripheries, as Vienna did with Budapest, and in time the empire may become a hybrid empire with various autonomous "kingdoms" and "principalities" that no longer respect the authority of the center as it had in the past.
14. Fatma Müge Göçek, "The Social Construction of an Empire: Ottoman State under Suleiman the Magnificent," in *Süleymân II and His Time*, ed. Halil İnalcık and Cemal Kafadar, 93–108 (Istanbul: Isis Press, 1993).
15. Mark R. Beissinger, "Demise of an Empire-State: Identity, Legitimacy, and the Deconstruction of Soviet Politics," in *The Rising Tide of Cultural Pluralism: The Nation-State at Bay?*, ed. Crawford Young (Madison: University of Wisconsin Press, 1993), 98, 99.
16. A point made eloquently by Mark Beissinger.
17. The distinction between ethnic group and nationality/nation need not be territory but rather the discourse in which they operate. The discourse about ethnicity is primarily about culture, cultural rights, and some limited political recognition, while the discourse of the nation is more often about popular sovereignty, state power, and control of a territorial homeland. But this is not necessarily or exclusively so, for one can conceive of non-territorial nationalisms, like those of the Jews before Zionism, the Armenians in the nineteenth century, and the Gypsies. For another view on the problems of definitions, see Lowell W. Barrington, "'Nation' and 'Nationalism': The Misuse of Key Concepts in Political Science," *PS: Political Science & Politics* 30, no. 4 (December 1977): 712–16.
18. See, for example, Etienne Balibar, "The Nation Form: History and Ideology," in *Race, Nation, Class: Ambiguous Identities*, ed. Etienne Balibar and Immanuel Wallerstein, 86–106 (London: Verso, 1991); Benedict Anderson, *Imagined Communities: Reflections on the Origin and Spread of Nationalism* (London: Verso, 1983).
19. Rogers Brubaker, *Citizenship and Nationhood in France and Germany* (Cambridge, MA: Harvard University Press, 1992), 22, 27.
20. Nation-states and empires can be seen as two poles in a continuum, but rather than fixed and stable, they may flow into one another, transforming over time into the other. A nation-state may appear stable, homogeneous, coherent, and yet with the rise of ethnic, sub-ethnic, or regionalist movements be perceived by sub-altern populations as imperial. For those identifying with the dominant population in Belgium, it is a nation-state, perhaps a multinational state, but for a Flemish militant who feels the oppression of the Walloon majority, Belgium is a kind of mini-empire. The term empire has been used polemically for small states like Belgium, Georgia, and Estonia, and it may seem anomalous to refer to such nationalizing states as empires. But it is precisely with the assimilating homogenizing, or discriminating practices of the nationalizing state that relationships of difference and subordination—here considered the ingredients of an imperial relationship—are exposed.
21. See Benedict Anderson's chapter on "Official Nationalism and Imperialism" in *Imagined Communities*, 83–112; and Jane Burbank, "Imperiia i grazhdanskoe obshchestvo: Imperskaia konstruktsiia Rossii i Sovetskogo Soiuza," in *Imperskii stroi Rossii v re-*

gional'nom izmerenii (XIX-nachalo XX veka), ed. P. I. Savel'ev, 19–35 (Moscow: Moscow Public Science Foundation, 1997).
22. On the Ottoman case, see Ronald Grigor Suny, "Religion, Ethnicity, and Nationalism: Armenians, Turks, and the End of the Ottoman Empire," in *In God's Name: Genocide and Religion in the Twentieth Century*, ed. Omer Bartov and Phyllis Mack, 23–61 (New York: Berghahn Press, 2001).
23. See, Frederick Cooper and Randall Packard, "Introduction," in *International Development and the Social Sciences: Essays on the History and Politics of Knowledge*, ed. Cooper and Packard, 1–41 (Berkeley: University of California Press, 1997).
24. Ibid., 3.
25. Marc Raeff, "Patterns of Russian Imperial policy Toward the Nationalities," in *Soviet Nationality Problems*, ed. Edward Allworth, 22–42 (New York, Columbia University Press, 1971); Raeff, "In the Imperial Manner," in *Catherine the Great: A Profile*, ed. Marc Raeff, 197–246 (New York: Hill & Wang, 1972); and S. Frederick Starr, "Tsarist Government: The Imperial Dimension," in *Soviet Nationality Policies and Practices*, ed. Jeremy Azrael, 3–38 (New York: Praeger, 1978).
26. Michael Khodarkovsky, "'Not by Word Alone': Missionary Policies and Religious Conversion in Early Modern Russia," *Comparative Study of Society and History* 38, no. 2 (April 1996): 267–93.
27. Yuri Slezkine, *Arctic Mirrors: Russia and the Small Peoples of the North* (Ithaca, NY: Cornell University Press, 1994), 47–71.
28. Quoted in Andreas *Kappeler, Russland als Vielvolkerreich: Entstehung, Geschichte, Zerfall* (Munich: C. H. Beck, 1993), 121; Richard Wortman, *Scenarios of Power: Myth and Ceremony in Russian Monarchy*, vol. 1: *From Peter the Great to the Death of Nicholas I* (Princeton: Princeton University Press, 1995), pp. 136–37.
29. Wortman, *Scenarios of Power*, 170.
30. Marc Szeftel, "The Form of Government of the Russian Empire Prior to the Constitutional Reforms of 1905–06," in *Essays in Russian and Soviet History in Honor of Geroid Tanquary Robinson*, ed. John Shelton Curtiss, 105–19 (New York: Columbia University Press, 1962).
31. Ibid., p. 230.
32. A. L. Zisserman, *Dvadtsat'piat let na Kavkaze, 1842–1867* (St. Petersburg, 1879), 1:10 for a discussion of Europeanization in Georgia, see N. G. Volkova and G. N. Dzhavakhishvili, *Bytovaia kul'tura Gruzii XIX–XX vekov: traditsii i innovatsii* (Moscow: Nauka, 1982), 185–95.
33. Joseph Davrichewy, *Ah! Ce qu'on rigolait bien avec mon copain Staline* (Paris: Éditions Jean-Claude Simoën, 1979), 53.
34. Ibid., 65, 69.
35. Mikhail Agursky, "Stalin's Ecclesiastical Background," *Survey* 28, no. 4 (Winter 1984): 2.
36. On Azerbaijan and the formation of an Azerbaijani identity in this period, see Tadeusz Swietochowski, *Russian Azerbaijan, 1905–1920: The Shaping of National Identity in a Muslim community* (Cambridge: Cambridge University Press, 1985); Aidyn Balaev, *Azerbaidzhanskie tiurki: protsessy formirovaniia natsii i natsional'noi identichnosti na rubezhe XIX–XX vv.* (Baku: Qanun, 2010).
37. Theorists of nationalism have long emphasized the importance of social communication

in the development of a sense of nation. Among the most important works in this genre are: Karl Deutsch, *Nationalism and Social Communication: An Inquiry into the Foundations of Nationality* (Cambridge, MA: MIT Press, 1953); Ernest Gellner, *Nations and Nationalism* (Oxford: Basil Blackwell, 1983); Benedict Anderson, *Imagined Communities: Reflections on the Origin and Spread of Nationalism* (London and New York: Verso Books, 1991). See also the review of views about nationalism by Geoff Eley and Ronald Grigor Suny, "Introduction: From the Moment of Social History to the Work of Cultural Representation," in *Becoming National, A Reader*, ed. Eley and Suny, 3–37 (New York: Oxford University Press, 1996).

38. Davrichewy, *Ah! Ce qu'on rigolait bien avec mon copain Staline*, 62–63.
39. See the chapter "Emancipation and the End of Seigneurial Georgia," in Ronald Grigor Suny, *The Making of the Georgian Nation* (Bloomington, IN: Indiana University Press, 1988, 1994), 96–112.
40. See, for example, the programmatic article by Petre Umikashvili, "sakhalkho simgherebisa da zghaprebis shekreba [The Collection of Folk Songs and Tales]," *droeba* 22 (1871); H. Paul Manning, "Describing Dialect and Defining Civilization in an Early Georgian Nationalist Manifesto: Ilia Ch'avch'avadze's 'Letters of a Traveler'," *Russian Review* 63, 1 (January 2004): 33.
41. Oliver Reisner, "Die georgische Alphabetisierungsgesellschaft: Schule nationaler Eliten und Vergemeinschaftung," *Jahrbücher für Geschichte Osteuropas* 48, no. 1 (2000): 66–89; Reisner, "The Tergdaleulebi: Founders of Georgian National Identity," in *Forms of Identity: Definitions and Changes*, ed. Ladislaus Löb, István Petrovics, and György E. Szonyi, 125–37 (Szeged, Hungary: Attila Jozsef University, 1994),; and Reisner, *Die Schule der Georgischen Nation: Eine sozialhistorische Untersuchung der nationalen Bewegung in Georgien am Beispiel der "Gesellschaft zur Verbreitung der Lese- und Schreibkunde unter den Georgiern" (1850–1917)* (Wiesbaden: Reichert Verlag, 2004).
42. For an extended treatment of the Georgian national movement, see James William Robert Parsons, "The Emergence and Development of the National Question in Georgia, 1801–1921" (PhD diss., University of Glasgow, 1987).
43. Il. Chavchavadze, "zogierti ram," *droeba* 24 (March 7, 1876); cited in Austin Jersild and Neli Melkadze, "The Dilemmas of Enlightenment in the Eastern Borderlands: The Theater and Library in Tbilisi," *Kritika* 3, no. 1 (2002): 38.
44. Kaminskii and Vereshchagin, "Detstvo i iunost' vozhdia," 49–50; Grishashvili, *Literaturnaia bogema starogo Tbilisi*, 18–20.
45. For an excellent discussion of this important work, see H. Paul Manning, "Describing Dialect and Defining Civilization," 26–47.
46. *Kvali* 22 (May 22, 1894).
47. Iveria or Iberia was the ancient Greek name for Eastern Georgia (Kartli in Georgian). Western Georgia was called Colchis by the Greeks and Imereti by the Georgians.
48. *Moambe*, 1894, nos. 5-6. For more complete discussions of the conflicts in Georgian intellectual life at the end of the nineteenth century, see Parsons, "The Emergence and Development of the National Question in Georgia," 298–321; and Suny, "The Emergence of Political Society," *The Making of the Georgian Nation*, 113–43.
49. *Moambe*, 1894, nos. 5-6.
50. Grigorii Uratadze, *Vospominaniia gruzinskogo sotsial-demokrata* (Stanford: Hoover Institution, 1968), 11.

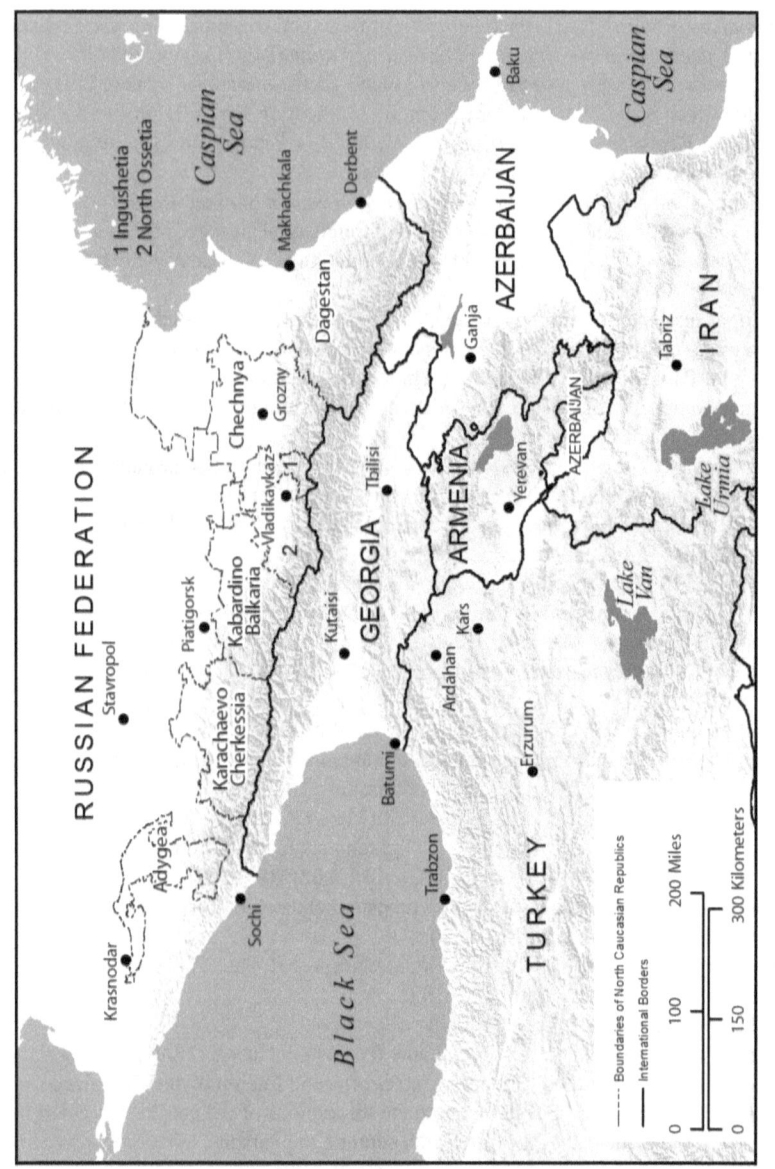

The Caucasus Today

Islam and Political Violence in Post-Soviet Daghestan: Discursive Strategies of the Sufi Masters

MICHAEL KEMPER AND SHAMIL SHIKHALIEV*

On 28 August 2012, the eminent Naqshbandiyya and Shadhiliyya shaykh Sa'id-Afandi al-Chirkavi (Said-afandi Atsaev, b. 1937) was assassinated in his house in the Avar village of Chirkey in the Daghestani mountains; six more people died in this attack of a female suicide bomber. Said-Afandi was the most authoritative Sufi leader of Daghestan, and the most prominent Sufi master in the whole Russian Federation. He was also seen as the grey eminence behind the Daghestani Muftiate (the Spiritual Administration of the Muslims of Daghestan, DUMD), and reportedly had thousands of followers and many personal disciples in Daghestan and beyond. The perpetrator, a young Muslim woman, obviously came from the camp of the Islamic underground cells (the "brothers in the forests") in Daghestan that have been offering violent resistance against the authorities for years. Most observers agree that Said-Afandi was killed for his strong criticism of what he used to call "Wahhabism," that is, of Salafi trends that oppose the Russian state, the Daghestani republican elites, and the state-supported Islamic establishment in the North Caucasus.

---

* This paper was written in the framework of two projects: "Jadidism in Daghestan: Muslim Modernism between the Middle East and Russia," funded by the Gerda-Henkel Foundation (Shikhaliev), and "The Russian Language of Islam," supported by the Dutch Scientific Organisation (Kemper).

In Daghestan, where assassinations and armed clashes occur on an almost daily basis,[1] such political violence against highest Islamic authorities is rampant—some sources count 35 victims over the past few years. Other prominent Sufi masters who were assassinated include Sirazhuddin Israfilov (27 October 2011) and Il'ias Khadzhi Il'iasov (3 August 2013), both not from Said-Afandi's Mahmudiyya group but from the second wing of the Naqshbandiyya in Daghestan, the Khalidiyya. Mosque imams and professors of Islamic teaching institutes have also been also targeted.[2]

In other parts of the Russian Federation, such killings of Islamic authorities have occurred as well. In the same summer of 2012, on 19 July, the deputy mufti of the Tatarstani Muftiate (DUMRT), Valiulla Iakupov, was shot dead in his house in Kazan, while his superior, Tatarstan's Mufti Il'dus Faizov, barely escaped a parallel bomb attack. While Valiulla Iakupov was not openly linked to a Sufi brotherhood, he was also regarded as the major conceptual thinker behind the pro-Kremlin Muftiate, and as a fierce critic of "Wahhabism."[3]

Against "Wahhabism," the official Islamic authorities defend what they call "Islamic traditionalism," that is, a conservative trend emphasizing the authority of the venerated Islamic Sunni legal schools (*madhhab*s), especially Shafi'ism and Hanafism. These legal schools had emerged in the Arab world of the eighth and ninth centuries and shaped Islam in huge parts of the Muslim world; since the medieval period the Shafi'i school has been dominant in the North East Caucasus, and Hanafism among the Tatars of the Volga area. Accordingly, the curricula of Islamic education in these areas were strongly shaped by Shafi'i and Hanafi textbooks from the Middle East and, in the case of Tatar Hanafism, from Central Asia.

In the case of Daghestan, the defense of the "traditional" Shafi'i school of law (and Ash'ari theology) goes hand in hand with the defense of Sufism, and in particular of the Naqshbandiyya Khalidiyya Mahmudiyya. As will be shown below, this Sufi brotherhood (*tariqa*) became the most prominent and wide-spread Sufi brotherhood in the post-Soviet republic.

In this article we will analyze the publication strategies of the Daghestani Naqshbandiyya Mahmudiyya Sufis in the face of their Islamic opponents by studying the Mahmudiyya's literary production. This Mahmudiyya discourse is highly political: the shaykhs have control over the state-supported Islamic institutions in Daghestan, and their brand of Islam is widely privileged by the state as a major ideological bulwark against "Wahhabism" and Islamic militancy. At the same time the Mahmudiyya discourse is also deeply historical, with Sufi (and political) legitimacy constructed through models and heroes of the past, and through Islamic conceptualizations of continuity over the centuries. After a survey of how the Mahmudiyya rose to prominence in Daghestan, we will focus on two genres that dominate the publications of the Mahmudiyya in Daghestan today, namely (1) anti-"Wahhabi" polemics and (2) historical self-representations of the Mahmudiyya Sufis (which we will discuss as a new genre of "post-Soviet hagiographies"). As some of the works of the grand master Said-Afandi himself have been studied in another paper,[4] we will focus here on the writings of other Mahmudiyya authors, among whom we find a certain distribution of tasks in the overall media strategy of the Mahmudiyya brotherhood. Beyond the scope of this paper is the Mahmudiyya's use of electronic media; the latter, however, is largely following the discourse as outlined in printed materials.

The Rise of the Mahmudiyya in Soviet and Post-Soviet Daghestan

The Naqshbandiyya khalidiyya has two branches in Daghestan: one that is usually simply referred to as the "Khalidiyya," and another that defines itself as the "Khalidiyya Mahmudiyya," or just the "Mahmudiyya." Both branches lead their spiritual line of transmission back to Isma'il al-Kurdamiri (d. 1277/1860–61) from what is today Northern Azerbaijan; Kurdamiri was a disciple of Mawlana Khalid al-Baghdadi (d. 1827), the Kurdish founding father of the Khalidiyya suborder of the Naqshbandiyya brotherhood. The two branches of Khalidiyya and Mahmudiyya thus share most of their "spiritual genealogy" (*silsila*) but differ in various respects.

First, the Khalidiyya had close ties to the first and the third of the three Daghestani imams who led the Islamic resistance against the Russian colonial encroachment in Daghestan and Chechnya, Ghazi-Muhammad (ruled as Imam from ca. 1828 to his death in battle in 1832) and the famous Imam Shamil (ruled 1834–59; died 1871 in exile in Medina). Ghazi-Muhammad regarded himself as a disciple of two major shaykhs of the Khalidiyya,

Kurdamiri's disciple Muhammad al-Yaraghi (d. 1838) and the latter's disciple, Jamaladdin al-Ghazighumuqi (d. 1866); al-Ghazighumuqi was also a close spiritual advisor to Imam Shamil. In Russian and Western historical literature, Shamil's Imamate is often explained through the concept of *"muridism,"* which implies that Shamil ruled and fought with the help of *murid*s (Sufi adepts), or through warriors that were as obedient to Shamil as *murid*s are supposed to be towards their Sufi masters; some scholars even depict the whole Imamate and its *jihad* against the Russians as based on Sufi networks.[5] There are good reasons to assume that this was not the case—we have no documentary evidence from the Imamate period for the assumption that Shamil was regarded, or regarded himself, as a Sufi shaykh in his own right. Furthermore, from the Daghestani Arabic-language documentation of Shamil's reign we know that Sufis played no important role in the administration or the military of the Imamate (in which Shamil employed representatives of various elites, including defectors from the old aristocracies as well as "new" Islamic scholars). Still, the fact remains that the Khalidiyya shaykhs became associated with the *jihad* of Ghazi-Muhammad and Shamil.[6] By contrast, the Mahmudiyya branch—named after Isma'il al-Kurdamiri's other disciple Mahmud al-Almali (d. 1877) from the village of Almali, today also in Northern Azerbaijan—was not linked to the Imamate and seems to have opposed Shamil's *jihad* against the Russians.[7] This first major difference between the two branches is thus historical, and we will return to these early networks later in this paper.

The second difference concerns questions of Sufi techniques. In the early twentieth century, the Mahmudiyya had some prominent representatives who produced a significant amount of Sufi literature. The most important shaykhs were Sayfallah-Qadi Bashlarov (1853–1919), an ethnic Lak with a special interest in medicine,[8] as well as the latter's disciple, shaykh Hasan al-Qahi (1852–1937) from the village of Kakhib in the Avar region of Gidatl'. Under these two shaykhs the Mahmudiyya integrated elements from another Sufi brotherhood, the Shadhiliyya; this *tariqa* has its historical mainstay in North Africa and had previously not been home to Daghestan. The curious incorporation of Shadhiliyya practices into the Naqshbandiyya Mahmudiyya in early twentieth-century Daghestan resulted in a new system, according to which Mahmudiyya shaykhs would teach Shadhiliyya practices (especially the "loud" *dhikr*, that is, the vocal remembrance of Allah) to new adepts, while the core Naqshbandiyya methods (especially the "silent" *dhikr* and the spiritual connection between shaykh and *murid* called *rabita*) were transmitted only to their intimate disciples who had already progressed along the path and completely devoted their lives to Sufism. This combination opened up a wider toolkit for attracting many *murid*s at a beginners' level, and thus to spread the influence of the shaykhs to wider circles.[9] The integration of Shadhiliyya elements also led to a further differentiation from the mainstream Khalidiyya in Daghestan, with whom the Mahmudiyya got engaged in polemics about Sufi practice and about the veracity of their spiritual lines of transmission, the *silsila*s.

Both Naqshbandiyya groups suffered heavily in the early Soviet period, when many Sufi masters were either killed or exiled. Bashlarov perished in the Civil War;[10] and Hasan al-Qahi was executed by the Soviets in 1937. But Qahi's son Muhammad-ʿArif (1900–1977) and a few others of his disciples survived and continued the Sufi lineage, probably with little opportunities to attract new adepts. After the Second World War, the Mahmudiyya (or Mahmudiyya-Shadhiliyya) was therefore still limited in scope,

Sayfallah-Qadi Bashlarov (1853–1919). This photo, probably taken in his last years, is being widely used by Mahmudiyya/Shadhiliyya adherents for the Sufi technique of *rabita*: concentrating on his outward appearance, the *murid* establishes a spiritual link to Bashlarov. The rabita is characteristic for the Naqshbandiyya khalidiyya in general (from which the Mahmudiyya is an offshoot), and goes back to Mawlana Khalid; the use of photographs is so far however only documented for the Daghestani Mahmudiyya. Said-Afandi approved it for the *rabita* to the great Mahmudiyya founding fathers but claimed that he called on his students not to use photos when establishing *rabita* with himself.

centered on the Kakhib district (*raion*)[11] of the Daghestan Autonomous Soviet Socialist Republic, with some representatives in villages of the Avar *raion*s of Khunzakh and Gumbet. By contrast, the Khalidiyya still had many representatives in several Avar and Kumyk regions of Daghestan.[12]

In the second half of the Soviet period the spread of Sufi affiliations got another boost through, paradoxically, Soviet agricultural policies. In the 1950s to 1970s, Soviet resettlement campaigns brought whole village populations from the poor Avar and Lak mountains to the fertile plains of Daghestan, which were historically the lands of the Kumyks. The goal was to break up the close-knit ethnic and Sufi networks by establishing big *kolkhoz*es in the plains. Yet what occurred was the opposite: the new *kolkhoz*es often preserved the original ethnic composition, and with these migrations also Sufi lineages were brought from the mountains to the lowlands, including into areas that were not directly touched upon by resettlement. Especially the Khalidiyya benefitted from this process, with Dargin shaykh Mukhammad-Amin Gadzhiev (1916–98) establishing his authority in the Kumyk raions of Kaiakent and Karabudakhkent, and others in the northern regions of Daghestan, among the Kumyks of Khasaviurt, Kiziliurt, and Babaiurt *raion*s. Among Gadzhiev's Kumyk disciples we find Mukhammad-Mukhtar Babatov (b. 1954), an influential imam who first worked in Tarki and then, from 1990, in Kiakhulai (both near Makhachkala).

The Mahmudiyya also saw an extension of its sphere of influence, though to a lesser degree. One important Mahmudiyya personality who served as a bridge between Mahmudiyya communities in the mountains and in the coastal plains was Mukhammad-Afandi Saaduev (Muhammad Saʿaduhajji, 1915–95) from the Avar mountain village of Batlukh, who established himself in Buinaksk, located at the foothills. Similarly, Mukhammad al-Khuchadi (from the Avar village of Khuchada in Kakhib raion) settled in Nechaevka, close to Kiziliurt in the north. In addition, with the Khalidiyya transferring its center of gravity from the mountains to the plains, the Mahmudiyya was able to strengthen its positions in the mountains. Still, by the end of the Soviet period the Mahmudiyya was still behind the Khalidiyya in terms of numbers and areas of influence. Yet with Saaduev and Khuchadi (and later with Said-Afandi, who studied with both of them) the Mahmudiyya had a number of charismatic leaders.[13]

Yet the major event that propelled the Mahmudiyya to dominance came in 1992, when the Soviet Muftiate for the North Caucasus (DUMSK, located in Daghestan's capital Makhachkala but also in charge of the other North Caucasus autonomous Soviet republics) fell apart according to ethno-national lines. Not only did Muftiates emerge in the neighboring republics of Russia's North Caucasus; also in Daghestan itself there were attempts to set up Islamic administrations based on ethnic markers (and linked to ethno-national movements that strove for autonomy within Daghestan).[14] While rival Muftiates popped up among the Kumyks, Dargins, and Laks, the central Daghestani Muftiate (now called DUMD, emerging from the Soviet DUMSK in Makhachkala) fell into the hands of the ethnic Avars, and particularly of Said-Afandi and his disciples. The competition with Islamic leaders of other ethnicities continued, but by 1994 the ethno-political movements were exhausted, and the rival "ethnic" Muftiates ceased to exist.[15] The Daghestani government supported the central Muftiate, in an attempt to use it as an ideological ally against the new major challenge, the rise of violent Salafi ("Wahhabi") groups. These groups had developed not only in Chechnya (where during and after the first Chechen War of 1994–96 national separatism had largely given way to Islamic ideologies) but also in northern Daghestan; and in the Dargin region of Kadar and Karamakhi, Islamic radicals even established an "independent Islamic territory" that existed for several years until the Russian army destroyed it in August 1999 (in the same month that Chechen groups made an incursion into Dagestan's Tsumada and Botlikh districts, in an attempt to link up with Daghestani Salafis, but were expelled by local Avar forces and the Russian Army—an event that triggered the second Chechen war).[16] One of the first prominent victims of Islam-motivated terrorist attacks was the Daghestani Mufti (and disciple of Said-Afandi) Said-Mukhammad Abubakarov (assassinated in August 1998). Abubakarov was replaced as Mufti by Akhmad-Hajji Abdulaev, another Avar *murid* of Said-Afandi, who is still in office and follows Said-Afandi's line. Officially, being a *murid* of Said-Afandi is not a prerequisite for working in the Muftiate, and in 2004 Abdulaev stated that from the 39 co-workers of his Muftiate, only 14 were Avars.[17] Yet in public perception the Muftiate is clearly seen as dominated by followers of Said-Afandi, and by Avars.[18]

The take-over of the Muftiate by Said-Afandi's disciples opened up new opportunities and resources for spreading their Mahmudiyya *tariqa*. Most of the ten to sixteen Islamic teaching institutes that emerged in Daghestan in the 1990s were directed by Said-Afandi's disciples;[19] the first to mention here is the Islamic Institute (named after the Mahmudiyya grandmaster Sayfallah Bashlarov, d. 1919) in the city of Buinaksk, which has been directed by Said-Afandi's *murid* Arslanali Gamzatov from Paraul. Makhachkala saw the opening of a prestigious new Friday mosque and of another teaching institute, the Daghestani Islamic University (named after Muhammad-'Arif, d. 1977, the son of the above-mentioned shaykh Hasan al-Qahi); this university is directed by the Mufti Abdulaev. These teaching institutions produced a significant number of graduates who were then sent to urban and village mosques in Daghestan, including into areas where the Mahmudiyya had not been seen before. In most of these areas local communities resented the new arrivals.[20] Equally important is that the Muftiate, and with it the Mahmudiyya and particularly Said-Afandi, have been in full control of the Islamic newspapers in the country (*Assalam, Nurul' Islam, Islamskii vestnik*) and the Islamic radio and TV programs; at present, the "media holding" of the Muftiate is directed by the wife of the current mufti, the journalist Patimat Gamzatova. These outlets popularize the positive image of the Mahmudiyya shaykhs and critique the "false shaykhs" in Daghestan, a term by which the shaykhs of the parallel Khalidiyya line is meant. At the same time the Muftiate is confronted with criticism in the secular

Said-Afandi from Chirkei (1937–2012) in the 1980s. Courtesy of Magomed Shekhmagomedov, disciple of Said-Afandi and co-worker at the Institute of History, Archeology and Ethnography, Makhachkala.

press for its inefficient handling of the Islamic pilgrimage to Mecca and Medina, which involves big money and which the Muftiate organizes in cooperation with private tourism companies. Equally widespread is the demand to include more representatives of other nationalities into DUMD and into Daghestan's Council of Alims (*Sovet alimov*), the body of Islamic scholars that elects the mufti. The complete Mahmudiyya monopoly on official religious resources has led to the disaffection also of many Islamic scholars of other nationalities whose loyalty to the government is generally not in question. Nonetheless, the government deems it too risky to embark on a reform of DUMD and continues to protect Said-Afandi's structures.[21]

In view of this politicization of Sufism, Said-Afandi presented himself as the grey eminence. He published his scholarly writings and appeared in the media but refrained from accepting any official functions in the expanding Islamic institutional establishment, which he controlled informally, through shaykh-student relations. The circle of his closest disciples seems to have remained small. One of his most active followers has been the Kumyk Arslanali Gamzatov from Paraul (b. 1956), who was crucial for expanding the Shadhiliyya (as the secondary and "lower" part of the Mahmudiyya-Shadhiliyya combination) into non-Avar regions of Daghestan. Gamzatov had first been a disciple of the Kumyk Muhammad-Amin Gadzhiev, a master of the "rival" Khalidiyya branch, but in the early 1990s he switched to the Avar Said-Afandi, who after just a few years made Arslanali Gamzatov his deputy in the Shadhiliyya brotherhood. Gamzatov quickly became director of the Bashlarov Islamic Institute in Buinaksk, where he produced the imams that were then sent via DUMD out to local mosques not only in the Kumyk-populated Buinaksk area but also among the Kumyks of northern Daghestan and partly even in the Lezgi lands in the south. At the same time he served as chairman of the Council of Alims, giving it a non-Avar face. Yet as Arslanali-Afandi's authority grew, Said-Afandi downgraded his status by revoking the Shadhiliyya license that he had granted him before. Almost all of Gamzatov's disciples went over to Said-Afandi or to Abduldzhalil (b. 1943) from Verkhnii Karanai (Buinaksk raion), whom Said-Afandi now promoted as his preferred successor.[22] Abduldzhalil is, like Said-Afandi, an ethnic Avar.

When Said-Afandi was assassinated in the summer of 2012 it was indeed Abduldzhalil who took over leadership of the Mahmudiyya and Shadhiliyya. Arslanali Gamzatov, by contrast, does not figure anymore in the official "spiritual genealogies" published by DUMD. He is treated as a "scholar" (*'alim*), not as a Sufi master, and has also lost the title "afandi," which is the Daghestani honorific of a Sufi master.[23] Yet Abduldzhalil does not yet have the public authority that Said-Afandi wielded; he is still in the shadow of his former master. By making a distinction between licenses on Naqshbandiyya and Shadhiliyya level, Said-Afandi seemed to be using the latter as an instrument to recruit followers from among Kumyks, Dargins, and others, while the Mahmudiyya "core" remained reserved for ethnic Avars.[24]

Anti-Wahhabi Polemics

Looking beyond the inner-Sufi tensions, the major enemies of the Mahmudiyya establishment are the Salafi-minded groups of various shades and colors. These include the so-called Caucasus Emirate (*Emirat Kavkaz*) that was led by the Chechen underground Islamist Dokku Umarov (killed in the summer of 2013), who claimed to have authority not only over the remaining Islamic cells operating in Chechnya but also over the various Caucasian "fronts" and "provinces" (*vilayats*), including the *vilayat* of Daghestan.[25] In Daghestan, the group that is most prominent in the media is this *Vilayat Dagestan* group. It has its own websites and claims to have executed major terror attacks, including the Volgograd bombings of December 2013. Yet such public self-attributions can scarcely be verified, and there are good reasons to assume that the Caucasus Emirate is largely a fiction, maintained by its Western-based website where Dokku Umarov (or now his successors) can only react to events, and do not direct them.

We must assume that in Daghestan, there are several radical networks at work that at times cooperate but also compete with each other. Radical Islamists also participate in the extortion of businessmen and can barely be distinguished from the "normal" racketeer and banditry/corruption networks.[26] In the villages, young Muslims might have many personal reasons to join the "brothers in the forests," in addition to the social, economic and political problems that social scientists usually refer to when they try to explain the emergence of youth radicalism.[27]

What is perhaps more important to note is that beyond the media-savvy terrorists, we observe a much broader trend towards Islamic conservatism and moderate fundamentalist approaches in Daghestan. What unites this complex movement is that it is firmly rooted in the Daghestani tradition of Shafi'i Islamic law, but that it gives precedence to Quran and Sunna in cases when scholars see a conflict between their Shafi'i framework and the holy texts. We therefore suggest to subsume this movement under the uneasy term "Shafi'i fundamentalism," whereby "fundamentalism" stands for the strong reliance on the "fundamental" texts of Islam. Importantly, this movement of Salafi-oriented Shafi'ism is in opposition to the government, DUMD and the Mahmudiyya, but "Shafi'i fundamentalists" maintain that they refrain from political violence in Daghestan.

Within this movement we can distinguish three different groupings, largely by their attitudes towards Sufism:

First, "Shafi'i fundamentalism" includes some of the prominent Khalidiyya shaykhs, including the Kumyk Mukhammad-Mukhtar Babatov (referred to above) and the Dargin Mukhammad-Hajji Gadzhiev, the son of above-mentioned Khalidiyya shaykh Mukhammad-Amin Gadzhiev. Note that other Khalidis, in particular Il'ias-Hajji Il'iasov and Sirazhuddin Israfilov, argued for a constructive cooperation with the state—but both were assassinated in 2011 and 2013, respectively.

Second, among the "Shafi'i fundamentalists" we also find ethnic Dargin scholars (that is, specialists in Islamic law and theology, *'alim*s not Sufis) who respect Sufism in general but who argue that the last legitimate Daghestani Sufi shaykh was the Dargin 'Ali-Hajji Akushinskii (d. 1929)—which means that they reject all contemporary Daghestani Sufi masters, whether Mahmudiyya/Shadhiliyya or Khalidiyya.[28]

And third, there are youth congregations (*jama 'at*s) of "Shafi'i fundamentalists," many of whom have studied in the Middle East, particularly in Syria and Egypt, and who promote strict adherence to Shafi'i law with a certain room for *ijtihad* (legal reasoning by analogy). These youth communities reject the Russian authorities, DUMD, and the Sufi shaykhs of all colors (especially if they cooperate with the state), and see the caliphate as the only legitimate political system. And while they support the armed struggle against the Asad regime in Syria (in which some of them undoubtedly participate), they claim that they do not support the Salafi violent underground in Daghestan, the "brothers in the forests," which they loathe.[29]

The political authorities and the Muftiate label all of these oppositional groups as "Wahhabis," a term that is therefore becoming equivalent to "Islamic opposition to the state and to the state-supported and state-supporting Islamic institutions," regardless of which trend and whether violent or not. In Daghestan, using the label is a weighty accusation because Wahhabism has been officially outlawed in the republic since 1999.[30] The Mahmudiyya's anti-"Wahhabi" discourse is therefore congruent with state policy. Second, the identification of all Salafi (or, to use a more common term, "fundamentalist") enemies as "Wahhabis" links them to foreign activists, predominantly from the Gulf states. This reductionist explanation of the complex phenomenon of Salafism of course misses the point that the Salafi-oriented groups in Daghestan are, for the most part, home-grown communities that emerged in Daghestan itself as part of a reaction to decidedly Daghestani problems. Against this depiction of Salafism as a "foreign import," Salafi-minded indigenous authors stress the long history of Salafi ideas in Daghestan, the beginnings of which they trace back to the eighteenth century.[31]

Yet the identification of all Salafi opponents as "Wahhabis" (which belongs in quotation marks, as it is a polemical term) opens the path for a theological engagement with the historical teachings of Wahhabism (without quotation marks); this enables the Daghestani Mahmudiyya to draw from anti-Wahhabi discourses from the wider Muslim world. They then apply these inside Daghestan, portraying the Mahmudiyya as the champion of the true Islamic tradition against all others who are disqualified as evil enemies of Islam, that is, as "Wahhabis."

A second historical precedent for the contemporary dispute between Sufis and Salafis/"Wahhabis" relates to Daghestan's own history and goes back to the late imperial and early Soviet periods. Starting in the late nineteenth century, Muslim modernism (Jadidism) emerged in Daghestan.[32] Its major representatives stood for educational reform (including the introduction of "secular" sciences), which often went hand in hand with a critique of "irrational" elements of current Islamic practice that the Jadids considered as illegitimate, that is, as not in accordance with the sources of Islam, Quran, and Sunna, which many Jadids approached from a scientific and historical point of view. The major target of the Jadids' critique was

Sufism, with its cult of saints and tomb veneration, spiritual healing, and other miracles. Against this the Jadids posed a sober interpretation of Islam that was to be in conformity with science and modernity. Among the Jadid critics who openly criticized Sufism were Muhammad 'Abd al-Rashid al-Harakani (1900–1927), Muhammad 'Umari al-Ukhli (1901 to early 1940s), and Mas'ud from Mogokh (1893–1941); the latter two perished in Soviet camps or exile. Also Abu Sufyan Akaev (1872–1931, who too died in a camp) as well as Ali Kaiaev (1878–1943, died in exile in Kazakhstan) and his disciple Magomed-Saiid Saidov (1902–1985, who eventually made a career as an Arabist in Makhachkala's Institute of History, Archaeology and Ethnography) were very negative towards the Sufis, who, in their opinion, were unbelievers.[33] In the Soviet period, many elements of the Jadids' critique of Sufism were continued by the antireligious propaganda of the Communist Party (especially after 1945), but, of course, now from an atheist position.[34] Interestingly, the Sufis reacted to these accusations by identifying their Jadidi critics as "Wahhabi" in nature. That is, already in the early twentieth century the enemies of the Naqshbandis were brought into connection with the Wahhabiyya.[35]

While these historical antecedents are clear and available for referencing, today's defenders of Sufism avoid mentioning these earlier Daghestani debates. The reason for this omission is that this would place their contemporary enemies close to the stance of the Jadidi modernists, who are quite respected for their efforts to modernize Islamic education and for their experience of repression under Stalin. Furthermore, if contemporary Sufi masters referred to the nineteenth- and early twentieth-century Jadids as "Wahhabis" they would undermine their general claim that today's "Wahhabism" in Daghestan is the product only of recent foreign intrusion.

For this reason the Sufi authors prefer to cite mainly historical critiques of Wahhabism that originate from the Arab world. One source of arguments, for example, is found in the corpus of the well-known Mufti of Mecca Ahmad Zayni Dahlan (d. 1884).[36] In Said-Afandi's writings, for example, a central position is given to the claim that Wahhabis adhere to an anthropomorphic interpretation of Allah (based on the Wahhabis' reading of the famous Throne verse in the Quran, which mentions that God "sat down" on the throne).[37]

This point is also most prominent in the works of Kuramukhammad Ra-

Magomed-Saiid Saidov (1902–85) in the manuscript section of the Institute of History, Archeology and Ethnography, 1970s. By courtesy of Saidov's daughter Rabiiat.

mazanov (born 1956, assassinated in 2007), the Mahmudiyya scholar to whom we owe the most detailed critiques of "Wahhabism." Ramazanov served as chairman of the Daghestani Muftiate's "canonical department" (sic!, *kanonicheskii otdel*), an organ to control Islamic publications. For Ramazanov, "Wahhabism" is the attempt to destroy Islam "from within," by "distorting the true meaning of the Quran and the *hadith*s."[38] In his 2007 brochure entitled *Be Careful: Wahhabism!*, Ramazanov gives a long list of the distortions Wahhabis have inflicted upon Islam: next to their opinion that Allah "has organs" he blames them for their view that Muslims may not invoke the Prophet Muhammad to intercede on their behalf with Allah (the practice of *shafa'a*), and that they even forbid excessive praise of the Prophet (as is practiced in Sufi ritual). Another error of the Wahhabis is, according to Ramazanov, their heretic view that Muhammad did not see Allah when he ascended to the heavens on the *Mi'raj* journey mentioned in the Quran. Ramazanov then criticizes the Wahhabis for their destruction of several tombs of the Prophet's companions in Mecca and Medina, including that of Muhammad's first wife Khadija; and he attacks them for their rejection of the power of saints (*awliya'*, to whom Wahhabis emphatically do not assign any power of blessing and miracles) and of Sufism in general, including the Sufi practices of *dhikr* (collective remembrance of Allah). Ramazanov furthermore condemns the Wahhabis for rejecting all Sunni legal schools (*madhhab*s) and blames them for violating the Islamic consensus on questions of prayer ritual. With their practice of *takfir*, the Wahhabis declare all Muslims who do not follow the Wahhabi interpretations as unbelievers; this allows them to use violence against their Muslim opponents, which they justify as *jihad*.[39] What we see here is that Ramazanov's critique of Wahhabism is grounded in events of eighteenth-century Arabia, where Wahhabism indeed emerged as a violent movement; but as a characterization of Wahhabism in general, and of Wahhabi thought in contemporary Saudi Arabia, Ramazanov's points are grossly oversimplified and mistaken, and for characterizing Daghestan's contemporary Salafis they are of little value.

The second fascicle of Ramazanov's brochure is completely devoted to defending Sufism against Wahhabi accusations in the form of questions and answers. For each topic Ramazanov refers not just to Sufi writings (including those of Mahmudiyya shaykhs past and present) but especially to

Quranic verses and sayings of the Prophet, to counter the Wahhabis' claim that Sufism is not in accordance with these fundamental texts of Islam.[40] As he argues, all four Sunni *madhhab*s agree that "to turn to a true spiritual teacher [here: *nastavnik*, in the sense of personal Sufi master] is a duty of every person"; accordingly Sufism is not just permitted but even mandatory for Muslims.[41] Notable is that Ramazanov rejects Islamic violence only when it is committed by the "Wahhabis." In contrast, he extols the role of the Sufis who supported indigenous Muslim resistance against the Crusades and European colonialism, as in the case of the Daghestani *jihad* of Ghazi-Muhammad and Shamil, whom he depicts as masters of the Naqshbandiyya. In Ramazanov's view, today "90% of the Islamic activists in Daghestan are people of *tasawwuf*" (i.e., of Sufi brotherhoods),[42] a view that is certainly wishful thinking.

In his historical account of how the Wahhabis occupied Mecca and Medina, Ramazanov depicts the Wahhabis of the nineteenth century as instruments of British colonialist and imperialist policies. The destruction of Ottoman rule in Arabia and of the Islamic Caliphate was instigated by London, from where were sent "more than five thousands agents" who had all been trained in the Quran and in Arabic.[43] This claim that British intelligence "created" and orchestrated Muhammad ibn 'Abd al-Wahhab goes back to the fictional *Confessions of a British Spy*, which is an anti-British pamphlet attributed to an Ottoman author. A Russian translation of this obvious forgery has been circulating in Daghestan at least since 2000.[44] In Daghestan (as elsewhere in Russia), such accusations fit perfectly into the increasingly anti-Western public discourse, in which also Islamic authors feel very much at home. No wonder then that Ramazanov also attacks Westerners (from Karl Marx to the Orientalists Reynold A. Nicholson, d. 1945, and Louis Massignon, d. 1962) for their attempt to identify the origins of Sufism in pre-Islamic traditions, which in Ramazanov's view is a gross distortion of Sufism.[45] Ramazanov similarly attacks the academic Quran translations of contemporary scholars, like those of the Daghestani professional Arabist Nuri Osmanov and of the Russian convert to Islam, Valeriia Prokhorova.[46] Here his argument is that academic translations, with their attempt to stay as close to the text as possible, mislead the uneducated Muslims. This must be seen in the context of those parts of the Quran (of the later, Medinan period) which call for *jihad* against unbelievers. The Quran should therefore not be translated without a commentary that provides the necessary historical context. The underlying idea is that secular intellectuals play into the hands of "Wahhabism" because they share the "literalist" approach of historical Wahhabism. It seems in one media outlet Ramazanov directly attacked the Arabist Nuri Osmanov as a "Wahhabi," an absurd allegation that his boss, Mufti Abdulaev, later had to repair.[47]

Very important is also the style of how these arguments are presented, especially by references to widely respected Islamic authors of the previous centuries. After his violent death by a car bomb in July 2007, a book compiled to honor the memory of Ramazanov begins with a panegyric poem by Said-Afandi in which he compares Ramazanov to the medieval Shafi'i legal scholar Muhiyaddin Yahya al-Nawawi (d. 1277).[48] This theme of Ramazanov as the "Nawawi of our time" is then commented upon in detail by the compiler of the Ramazanov memorial publication, Magomedrasul Omarov (who is the press-secretary of the Daghestani Muftiate and a relative of the above-mentioned Mahmudiyya shaykh Mukhammad Saaduev from Batlukh, d. 1995). What is important here is that Ramazanov is presented not just as a devoted Sufi disciple of Said-Afandi but, more broadly, as a legal scholar well-versed in Quran and Sunna and in Islamic literature.

Ramazanov's role as the Mahmudiyya's "legal scholar" was taken over by Islam Makirdinovich Aiubov, who produced another comprehensive rejection of "Wahhabism", again with thousands of quotes from the Quran, the Sunna, the Shafi'i tradition, and the Mahmudiyya heritage. Interestingly, Aiubov's 2010 book, *Sufism and the Face of the Wahhabis*[49] (which the author dedicated to his spiritual preceptor Said-Afandi) appeared as a joint publication of DUMD and the Institute of History, Archeology and Ethnography of the Daghestani Center of the Russian Academy of Sciences; the academic credentials were added to increase the scholarly and scientific value of this work. However, the stamp of the Daghestani Academy of Sciences on the inner front page of the book was obviously used without approval of the Institute;[50] and in its scientific methodology Aiubov's book differs little from Ramazanov's works, in so far as it is an almost random sequence of quotes with a very limited scientific apparatus.

The current Mufti of Daghestan, Akhmed-Hajji Abdulaev (b. 1959), is also a disciple of Said-Afandi. After the latter's death Abdulaev positioned himself as a shaykh of both the Shadhiliyya and the Mahmudiyya (with a license that he reportedly obtained from Said-Afandi back in 2010, but that he kept secret until Abduldzhalil ordered him to "come out," and to take on *murid*s).[51] Not surprisingly, Mufti Abdulaev's published writings center on a defense of Sufism and an attack on "Wahhabism," again without any closer analysis about whom those Daghestani "Wahhabis" are supposed to be. An edition of his selected speeches (2010) displays the ambiguous situation in which the Muftiate finds itself. On the one hand Abdulaev stresses his independence from state organs and calls upon his mosque imams to not make propaganda for this or that politician in times of elections; but on the other hand Abdulaev also stresses the good relations between his Muftiate and the Daghestani state and does not hide his own participation in the meetings of the government's anti-terror agencies.[52] Like Ramazanov, Abdulaev is also in conflict with some academic researchers, whose publications on the Islamic situation in Daghestan he regards as a "provocation."[53]

Altogether, the Muftiate's publications are extremely vague about the rise of violent Islamic Salafism in the region; they all avoid mentioning names of their opponents (only well-known Wahhabis from Saudi Arabia are mentioned), and they lump them all together into one group, drawing no distinctions between groups that use violence and those that remain quietist. While at times acknowledging the importance of social and economic problems for the rise of Islamic extremism, all of these publications link the rise of "Wahhabism" to the lack of Islamic knowledge among the broader population. From this accusation of ignorance ensues the mission of "public enlightenment" that the Muftiate claims for itself. This approach—to explain Salafism by ignorance—must be highly offensive to the opponents, many of which have studied at first-rank Islamic institutes abroad. In other words, these anti-Wahhabi publications, designed as "prophylactic enlightenment work," are not meant to establish a dialog; they seek to address primarily their own constituency and to secure the state's support for the existing "official" Islamic establishment. On the other side, one can also surmise that beating historical Wahhabism and avoiding engagement with any specific, Daghestani opponent might be a strategy to avoid direct retaliation, however unsuccessful.

Yet a significant change was underway in 2012, when DUMD (with the blessing of Said-Afandi[54] and obviously after consultation with the state organs) opened negotiations with Islamic oppositionists, in particular with the Ahl al-Sunna Association. This organization reportedly represents some 60 to 70 Islamic scholars (of various ethnic backgrounds) of what we referred to above as "Shafi'i fundamentalism." Meetings in March and April 2012 resulted in a joint "Resolution", which identified following the Quran and Sunna and respect for the four legal schools as the smallest common denominator. According to the published version of the document, Muslims should not abuse and defame each other, Islamic missionary work should go unhampered, and Daghestani Muslims should not be hindered when they want to go abroad for studying. The "Resolution" envisaged the establishment of a joint organ composed of DUMD and Ahl al-Sunna on an equal base.[55] The underlying idea of this rapprochement between the Muftiate and Ahl al-Sunna was obviously that the latter would somehow be able to also influence the more radical Islamic militants and make them peaceful. Nothing came out of this, however: the negotiations were already overshadowed by the assassination on 23 March 2012 of Mukhammad Abdulgafurov, a theologian and imam of the Mahmudiyya stronghold of Buinaksk. With Said-Afandi's assassination on 28 August (from which Ahl al-Sunna has distanced itself) the dialog seems to have ended. We must assume that the termination of the dialog was the purpose of Said-Afandi's elimination; and the fact that the killing of Said-Afandi has not been properly investigated (like so many earlier cases) feeds rumors that some state organs might not be too unhappy about this course of events.

Mahmudiyya Hagiographies

Next to defenses against "Wahhabi" accusations, the Mahmudiyya also published numerous books about the history of their own *tariqa*; these works also have legitimacy production as their major purpose. The goal is to demonstrate the beneficial activities and piety of the Mahmudiyya shaykhs past and present, their service to the Muslim population, and their dedication to true Sufism, even in the face of Soviet oppression and now the "Wahhabi" threat. One central topic is the demonstration of unbroken chains of transmission from Mahmud al-Almali through Bashlarov and Hasan al-Qahi to the latter's son and further shaykhs, up to Said-Afandi.[56]

While most anti-"Wahhabi" publications are in Russian, the Daghestani Sufi literature is composed in various languages. The great Mahmudiyya masters of the late nineteenth and early twentieth centuries wrote in Arabic, and partly in Avar; and the Mahmudiyya shaykhs of our days, including Said-Afandi,[57] write in Avar. In order to reach out to a broader public these writings need to be translated into Russian, which is the only language available to all Daghestanis.

Editions and Translations of Arabic and Avar Works of Past Shaykhs

The most prestigious Mahmudiyya publications sold in local shops are the Arabic editions of the Sufi treatises and correspondences of the two central Mahmudiyya shaykhs of the late nineteenth and early twentieth centuries, Sayfullah Bashlarov (d. 1919) and Hasan al-Qahi (d. 1937).[58] Another major work published in this series is the fine Arabic collection of Sufi biographies from Daghestan written by Shaykh Shu'ayb Afandi al-Bagini (d. 1912) from the Avar village of Baginub.[59] This work presents a first history of the Mahmudiyya shaykhs up to Bagini's time, with extensive quotations from their works and with disparaging remarks about masters of the rival Khalidiyya branch. The Arabic editions of these works were printed in Syria, where there is still a sizable Daghestani community. It was Said-Afandi's disciple Arslanali Gamzatov who brought the Arabic manuscripts to Syria for publication.

Taken together, the Mahmudiyya shaykhs Bashlarov, Qahi and Bagini produced around twenty Sufi works between ca. 1880 and 1937, most of them in Arabic. This is an enormous contribution to the development of Sufi literature in Daghestan. For comparison, the total amount of non-Mahmudiyya Sufi works for the broader period of ca. 1820 to WWII, including the Khalidiyya, amounts to not more than about thirty.[60] It should, however, be added that before the Syrian editions came out, many of Mahmudiyya works existed only in the form of one or a few manuscripts, which reflects the limited outreach of the Mahmudiyya before the 1990s. The Khalidiyya writings, by contrast, were much more popular and can still be found in almost all Daghestani manuscript collections, owned by representatives of many different nationalities.

These full text editions have enormous significance for the contemporary Mahmudiyya in so far as they provide a detailed basis of information on their previous masters. Accordingly, Mahmudiyya authors constantly refer to this corpus of early Mahmudiyya Arabic writings. Yet for the average Daghestani reader these Arabic editions have only limited value. For many customers the purchase of these fine hard-cover books, we must assume, has above all symbolic value. More accessible are therefore the Russian translations of some of Hasan al-Qahi's works, one of them from the Arabic (a Sufi treatise addressed to his son Muhammad-'Arif)[61] and one from the Avar language.[62] Another Avar original work of Hasan al-Qahi, *Siraj al-sa'ada*, has been published in modern (Cyrillic) Avar.[63] Most of these translations and editions are rather professional, and were produced at the Bashlarov Islamic University in Buinaksk and other Mahmudiyya institutes. Yet these thick editions of historical works are still difficult to read, given the sometimes archaic language even in good Russian translation.

New Individual Hagiographies

More important for spreading knowledge about the lives and works of the Mahmudiyya shaykhs are therefore popular brochures and short booklets in the Russian language. The first of these was Magomed A. Amirkhanov's "World of Islam" of 1996, a pocket-format booklet that combined basic information on Islam with the first historical narrative of the Mahmudiyya shaykhs in Daghestan.[64] Amirkhanov continued this line of publications, also in Russian, with a series on individual Avar shaykhs of the Mahmudiyya, including two booklets on Shu'ayb Afandi al-Bagini and one on the latter's disciple Ibrahim al-Kuchri (who reportedly fought against the Bolsheviks, was imprisoned, and died in the late 1920s).[65] These and some similar booklets provide information on the biographies of the respective masters (including on their teachers), reproduce statements from their works and from oral lore, and mention their disciples. The booklet on Bagini includes long descriptions of the character and outward appearance of the Prophet Muhammad, obviously taken from Bagini's unpublished Avar-language poetic biography of Muhammad, *Qawa'id jawahir al-'ajam*. From the "founder" and namesake of the Mahmudiyya branch,

Mahmud al-Almali, there are no relevant original texts extant. His followers have reconstructed his life on the basis of later writings and oral transmission, in the form of another modern hagiography.66

We suggest that these writings represent a new unique genre that is best called "post-Soviet hagiography." The Daghestani Mahmudiyya cycle perhaps represents one of the largest corpora of this genre. Comparisons with similar works from Tajikistan, Kazakhstan, and other post-Soviet regions would be most helpful for identifying common and distinct features.67 For the case of the Mahmudiyya corpus we can already distinguish four major characteristics that distinguish this genre from classical Islamic hagiographies.68

First, these books provide highly detailed factual information. References to historical events taking place during the lives of the respective shaykh are not just left in the "background" but constitute major topics of the narratives. The information provided includes names of persons and places, years of meetings and deaths, and even descriptions of the construction of the shaykh's mausoleum (as a place of pilgrimage, *ziyara*). This style and type of content speak to post-Soviet readers interested in empirical facts, both because their Soviet and post-Soviet school education was oriented towards facts and figures, and because there was an acute lack of basic information on Islam in the 1980s and 1990s. Against this "factual information" the devotional purpose of such literature seems to be secondary.

A second feature of this post-Soviet genre is that the lives of the Daghestani shaykhs are embedded in a broader Islamic framework by many references to the Quran and the Prophet and by enriching the text with multiple quotations from famous Sufis of the classical period, from Junayd (d. 910), to Baha'addin Naqshband (d. 1389), to Hasan al-Qahi (d. 1937). The emphasis on the Quran is partly to be seen in the context of "Wahhabi" accusations that Sufism is not Islamic. Again, however, the reference to the holy texts and their "scientific" analysis in some of these hagiographies also speaks to the above-mentioned mindset of Islamic rationalism that ensued from Russian education. The goal is to demonstrate that Sufis are not the "obscurants" that Soviet atheist publications and post-Soviet Salafi critiques accuse them of being. Tellingly, particular Sufi techniques—like the Naqshbandiyya *rabita* and the *dhikr*—are only mentioned in passing;

detailed information on these practices can be obtained from another post-Soviet genre, that of questions and answers (represented, for example, in some of Said-Afandi's writings).[69]

Accordingly—and this is the third feature—these hagiographies give little room to miracles. Of course the shaykhs are described as bearers of Allah's *barakat* (blessing), but the manifestations thereof are rather modest. In Amirkhanov's 2007 account of Shu'ayb al-Bagini's life, for instance, the only "miracles" mentioned are that the shaykh was able to make other people see what can usually not be seen, as for instance a deceased relative. Similarly, one *murid* who provoked the shaykh by directly asking for a miracle suddenly feels he is in Medina (but immediately returns to the village). The reduced profile of miracles contrasts with the attention given to miracles by Shu'ayb al-Bagini in his own Arabic-language biographical dictionary (written in 1911). In that text some shaykhs (though not from the Mahmudiyya) could fly, and Mahmud al-Almali, the "founder" of the Mahmudiyya, had a conversation with a stone.[70]

Finally, these hagiographies certainly contain oral material but they are largely based on written texts, especially the above-mentioned Arabic-language works of the Mahmudiyya grandmasters of the early twentieth century and their Russian translations. What emerges is a network of cross-references, with multiple ties between various masters and disciples. By relying on one common corpus of writings, these post-Soviet hagiographies are serial, and interlinked. They have not grown over time but were compiled by identified authors, and the hagiographies on Bagini and Kuchri were produced by the same author in the same year of 2007. In contrast to the classical genre of hagiography, they are thus conscious constructions that largely follow the same pattern.[71]

What is striking is that all hagiographic narratives are taking place in rural environments—a feature that is also dominant in the classical hagiographic tradition. In the case of Daghestan, this is noteworthy because the large-scale urbanization and the ongoing migration into the cities, has not yet led to urban hagiographies. The village character of the Mahmudiyya hagiographies (which often include historical sections on the village of a given shaykh) seems to strike a chord with a general feeling of nostalgia for their ethnic mountain "homelands" that Daghestanis cherish. In this respect the Daghestani post-Soviet hagiographies are close to the equally

Mahmudiyya masters, probably in the early 1980s. Standing, from the left: Khasmukhammad Abubakarov (father of later Mufti Saiidmukhammad Abubakarov); next: Mukhammad Mansurov (disciple of Badruddin from Botlikh and Said-Afandi). Sitting, second from the left: Mukhammad Saaduev; third: Mukhammad Ibragim-Khalil from Tidib (1895–1985). Photo available on multiple internet sites.

flourishing genre of village histories (in which discussions of local Sufis also figure prominently, including with references to the Mahmudiyya publications).[72] While the village life of the past is remembered for its purity and spirituality, the contemporary cities are seen as oriented towards a secular and European lifestyle, with widespread corruption and moral degradation.

Collective Hagiographies

In addition to narratives on individual shaykhs we also find the genre of collective hagiographies. One fine example of this species is the book *The Golden Chain of the Naqshbandiyya Shaykhs*, published in 2004 by Mukhammad-Hajji Abdurakhmanov, a deputy mufti with a professional education in medicine.[73] This work comprises 30 short biographical entries on the Naqshbandiyya line from the Prophet Muhammad to Mawlana Khalid (d. 1827), followed by 25 entries on shaykhs who worked in Daghestan, from Khalid's disciple Kurdamiri to Badraddin from Botlikh who passed away in 1995. Noteworthy is that this latter "Daghestani" part (pp. 103–66) also includes three shaykhs who are part not of the Mahmudiyya line of transmission but are of the rival Khalidiyya, namely the masters of the Shamil period Muhammad al-Yaraghi, Jamaladdin al-Ghazighumuqi, and 'Abdarrahman al-Sughuri. Their inclusion can be seen, on the one hand, as an effort to give due recognition to these three well-known Khalidiyya masters who have an important place in Daghestani history. On the other hand, the omission of any of their Khalidiyya disciples supports the Mahmudiyya's claim that after the death of al-Sughuri in 1882, the Khalidiyya line was left without any respected shaykh.[74] The booklet is thereby a clear attempt to downgrade the rival Khalidiyya wing in present-day Daghestan and to present the Mahmudiyya as the only legitimate branch of the Naqshbandiyya in Daghestan.

A second example of such collective post-Soviet hagiographies is *Mountain Wisdom* (2009), a hard-cover book on colored pages, with many painted and photographic portraits. Its compiler, Magomedrasul Omarov, is introduced as the director of the "Information and Analytical Center *Fikr*", and as a member of the Union of Russia's Journalists. At the time of publication he reportedly followed a PhD track at the Institute of Language, Literature and Arts in Makhachkala.[75] Omarov's book contains only Daghestani shaykhs, beginning with Muhammad al-Yaraghi and Jamaladdin al-Ghazighumuqi. These are followed by the two *jihad* imams Ghazi-Muhammad and Shamil, whom it presents as Khalidiyya Sufi masters with full licenses from al-Yaraghi and/or al-Ghazighumuqi. Yet other shaykhs of the Khalidiyya wing (and even 'Abdarrakhman al-Sughuri) are omitted; the rest of the book is an account of the Mahmudiyya.

This compilation also goes further in time than the above-mentioned *Golden Chain* of 2004, in so far as Omarov also discusses Mukhammad-Afandi from Khuchada (1909–87, one of the masters of Said-Afandi) as well as Said-Afandi himself. It ends with Abduldzhalil-Afandi from Verkhnyi Karanai (b. 1943), thus already cementing Said-Afandi's selection of Abduldzhalil as his designated successor. As Omarov tells us, Abduldzhalil was first educated by other masters of the Mahmudiyya. Then, in 1995, shaykh Mukhammad-Afandi from Botlikh (who died in that very year) ordered Said-Afandi (who had been his disciple) to provide Abduldzhalil with a combined Naqshbandiyya (Mahmudiyya) and Shadhiliyya license (*ijaza*). Abduldzhalil, however, "kept this *ijaza* secret for 13 years." Only in 2009 did Said-Afandi command Abduldzhalil to take on *murid*s. In fact Said-Afandi transferred his own *murid*s "to the south of Chirkei" (which is Said-Afandi's native Avar village) to Abduldzhalil.[76] This investiture narrative and Abduldzhalil's late "coming out" are obviously related to Said-Afandi's decision to "take back" the Shadhiliyya *ijaza* that he had given to Arslanali Gamzatov, who before 2009 was regarded as Said-Afandi's preferred deputy and successor in Shadhiliyya affairs. Interesting to note is that Abduldzhalil is introduced here as a university-educated medical man and as chief doctor of a city hospital in Buinaksk. Abduldzhalil's disciple, Mukhammad Gadzhiev (editor of DUMD newspaper *Nurul' Islam*, and a relative of the prominent Mahmudiyya shaykh Saaduev, d. 1995), is also a medical professional.

Another novelty of *Mountain Wisdom* is that this work does not emphasize the factual biographies but rather focuses on short aphorisms attributed to the individual shaykhs. In the chapter on Said-Afandi, for example, we find statements like "Religion and state are like twins, you cannot feed the one without the other"; "The *mu'min* [believer] has three fortresses for defending himself from Satan: the mosque, the practice of *dhikr* [remembrance of Allah], and the reading of the Quran"; and "The *tariqa* [Sufi brotherhood] is a servant to the *shari'a* [Islamic law], that is, an instrument that decorates it."[77] These short sayings of the Mahmudiyya shaykhs have little specifically related to the social and historical environment of the North Caucasus. Still, by virtue of being classified under the title of "Mountain Wisdom", the Mahmudiyya masters are presented here as the incarnation of the Daghestanis' ethics and their true way of life, with the same sort of nostalgia for the lost village habitat.

Finally, beyond these Arabic, Avar, and Russian titles there are also some publications in the Dargin language. These too make full use of Hasan al-Qahi's Sufi writings. The author of most of these works was a Dargin *murid* of Said-Afandi, Gubdalan Abu Muslim, who served as imam in the Dargin village of Gubden. From 1994 until his passing away in 2007 Gubdalan Abu Muslim was also deputy mufti in Makhachkala. He produced a wide array of popular literature on Islam, from dogma, to ritual, to history. His Sufi booklets focus on the Shadhiliyya affiliations of Dargin shaykhs,[78] which confirms our impression that the non-Avars are largely limited to the "Shadhiliyya level."

Conclusion

In this paper we looked at the history of the Mahmudiyya in Soviet and post-Soviet Daghestan and analyzed their anti-"Wahhabi" polemical writings as well as their historical self-representation in the form of text editions and Sufi biographies/hagiographies. Both genres are deeply embedded in the history of the Mahmudiyya in Daghestan. In this conclusion we would like to bring the various threads together. We argue that while the Mahmudiyya and the Muftiate that it controls claim to be comprehensive and representative of all Daghestani Muslim nationalities, in fact their discursive strategies are highly partisan. While the unity of Islam is constantly referred to, the Mahmudiyya publications rather testify and contribute to the fragmentation of Islam in Daghestan.

The most striking feature of the anti-"Wahhabi" discourse of the Muftiate (DUMD) and the Mahmudiyya in general is of course that it labels all oppositional groups as "Wahhabis," a term that is therefore becoming equivalent to "Islamic opposition to Mahmudiyya, DUMD and state," regardless of which trend a group might represent and whether it is violent or not. In general, the routine anti-"Wahhabi" polemics of the Mahmudiyya strike us as missing the point. This raises the question why this discursive strategy is chosen and maintained at all costs.

One can indeed identify a number of advantages that come with this strategy. First, it allows the state-supported Islamic authorities to ignore the diversity of Islamic oppositional thought and to avoid any engagement with it (which might be a dangerous undertaking, for there are many highly-trained scholars also among the oppositionists). The extremely broad "Wahhabi foil"[79] projects all Islamic opposition in Daghestan as an import from the Middle East (and particularly from Saudi-Arabia, a country generally seen in Russia as a US satellite), as if all violence and all opponents subscribe to the tenets of Muhammad ibn 'Abd al-Wahhab (d. 1791) and his Wahhabi followers in Arabia. This reductionist explanation of the phenomenon of Salafism ignores the reality that the oppositional groups in Daghestan are, for the most part, home-grown communities that emerged in Daghestan itself and as a reaction to decidedly Daghestani problems. Indeed, we have seen that even the Dargin groups that we identified as "Shafi'i fundamentalists" present themselves as bearers of the true (historical) Daghestani way of Islam. Yet the Mahmudiyya authors' ignoring this *indigenous* character of the *contemporary* opposition and their presentation of all Islamic opposition as coming from the Middle East allow for a bashing of the *historical* forms of *Arab* Wahhabism, which is comparatively easy since many historical critiques of (Saudi) Wahhabism are readily available and can be employed.

Furthermore we demonstrated that with this discursive strategy, the contemporary Mahmudiyya shaykhs and writers follow the patterns of Mahmudiyya shaykhs of the first half of the twentieth century who referred to their Daghestani opponents from the Jadid camp as "Wahhabis." However, the contemporary Mahmudiyya writers do not openly acknowledge these Daghestani roots of their anti-"Wahhabism" discourse, since this would undermine their central argument that "Wahhabism" is only a recent intervention from abroad.

Polemics also permeate the numerous biographical/hagiographical works, in academic or popular forms, in which the Mahmudiyya authors depict the history of their own brotherhood. Next to the "Wahhabis," the major opponent here is the rival branch of the Khalidiyya, whose legitimacy the Mahmudiyya authors constantly reject on the grounds of their supposedly interrupted transmission lines and their faulty Sufi practices. As in the anti-"Wahhabi" writings, in these Sufi texts we also find a continuity from the early twentieth century through the Soviet period to the present day, which is reflected in the massive referencing of the two grand masters Hasan al-Qahi and Sayfallah Bashlarov in addition to Shu'ayb al-Bagini's comprehensive biographical account of the early Mahmudiyya. Their images indeed become larger than life; and the major Mahmudiyya teaching institutes bear the names of these Sufi giants.

This common corpus of the early twentieth century, now edited in the original Arabic and partly translated into Russian and Avar, gives the Mahmudiyya self-representation a strong and unified framework and provides a significant amount of continuity with, importantly, the pre-Soviet period. It depicts the Soviet era as an interlude in which the Mahmudiyya managed to preserve the original "mountain wisdom" that can now, finally, be taught without hindrance. At the same time, the massive production of Mahmudiyya hagiographical literature on Soviet-era shaykhs serves to obscure the fact that in the Soviet period the Mahmudiyya was still rather marginal compared to its rival, the Khalidiyya (which has so far produced only few hagiographical publications).[80]

The presentation of individual shaykhs follows the accounts of the early twentieth century not only in content but also in form. Characteristic is the strong emphasis on conformity with the Quran and Sunna. This has to be seen in the context of the critique of the Salafis who argue that the Sufis depart from the fundamentals of Islam and in fact became heretics. In this sense, the Mahmudiyya's anti-"Wahhabi" polemics and their self-representations form two sides of the same coin. At the same time, the references to the Quran and Sunna and the "sober" character of the miracles also speak to the Soviet-educated public at large, to followers who demand a rational approach to Islam and who would probably find more "supernatural" miracles less credible. This "scientific" inclination is also notable in the fact that several shaykhs have a professional background in medicine, from Bashlarov to the current head of the Mahmudiyya, Abduldzhalil.[81]

Finally, the sheer amount of Mahmudiyya publications and their overwhelming dominance in Daghestani Islamic book shops reflects the state's support in terms of funding (probably through the Muftiate) and the fact that their enemies, whether "Shafi'i fundamentalists" or Sufis of the rival Khalidiyya branch, have little access to legal print publications. We can assume that the Muftiate's "canonical department" (in cooperation with state organs) plays a role in averting publications that would challenge the position of the Mahmudiyya. Islamic oppositional writings are therefore largely restricted to electronic media and should be subject of a separate study.

The Mahmudiyya authors' linguistic strategies reflect their claim to represent all Daghestani nations. It should be noted that the official DUMD newspaper *Assalam* is indeed published in no less than seven Daghestani languages. And while most new texts are still composed in Avar (reflecting the reality that the Mahmudiyya is de-facto an Avar enterprise), significant efforts are made to translate these works, as well as the Arabic writings of earlier shaykhs, into Russian. To be sure, a few works are also produced in other Daghestani languages like Dargin and Kumyk, obviously in an attempt to spread the secondary Shadhiliyya part of the Mahmudiyya-Shadhiliyya group to non-Avars, but these remain marginal against the large body of publications in Russian, which is the chosen language for reaching out to non-Avars. It should be noted that the Russian publications of Said-Afandi and other Mahmudiyya authors also find markets outside of Daghestan. With his media strategies Said-Afandi in fact became the best known Sufi shaykh in the whole of the Russian Federation, and he also gained sympathies among Tatar Muslims, including those in Siberia,[82] and even among Russian converts to Islam.

In sum, the Mahmudiyya has separated itself from the rest of the Islamic spectrum in Daghestan with both its anti-"Wahhabi" publications and its historical self-representations. The Mahmuddiya and the state organs under its influence ignore or reject all other trends in the country. In the volatile multiethnic and diverse republic of Daghestan, this is a very dangerous policy, as can be seen from the heavy toll that Mahmudiyya leaders have had to pay for the privileged position that the government grants them.

Notes

1. John O'Loughlin, Edward C. Holland, Frank D.W. Wittmer, "The Changing Geogaphy of Violence in Russia's North Caucasus, 1999–2011: Regional Trands and Local Dynamics in Dagestan, Ingushetia and Kabardino-Balkaria," *Eurasian Geography and Economics* 52, no. 5 (2011): 1–35.

2. On Israfilov see Kimitaka Matsuzato and Magomed-Rasul Ibragimov, "Islamic Politics at the Sub-regional Level in Dagestan: Tariqa Brotherhoods, Ethnicities and the Spiritual Board," *Europe-Asia Studies* 57.5 (2005): 766–67. On Il'iasov, see Shamil Shikhaliev, "Sufiiskii sheikh segodnia," *Etnograficheskoe obozrenie* 2 (2006): 24–34.

3. Alfrid K. Bustanov and Michael Kemper, "Valiulla Iakupov's Tatar Islamic Traditionalism," *Asiatische Studien – Études Asiatiques* 67, no. 3 (2013): 809–35.

4. Michael Kemper "The Discourse of Said-Afandi, Daghestan's Foremost Sufi Master," in *Islamic Authority and the Russian Language: Studies on Texts from European Russia, the North Caucasus and West Siberia*, ed. by A. K. Bustanov and M. Kemper (Amsterdam: Uitgeverij Pegasus, 2012), 167–218.

5. For various interpretations that stress the role of Sufis in the *jihad* of the Imams, see Moshe Gammer, *Muslim Resistance to the Tsar: Shamil and the Conquest of Chechnia and Daghestan* (London: F. Cass, 1994); Anna Zelkina, *In Quest for God and Freedom: Sufi Responses to the Russian Advance in the North Caucasus* (London: Hurst, 2000); Michael Kemper, *Herrschaft, Recht und Islam in Daghestan. Von den Khanaten und Gemeindebünden zum ğihād-Staat* (Wiesbaden: Reichert, 2005); and Clemens P. Sidorko, *Dschihad im Kaukasus: Antikolonialer Widerstand der Dagestaner und Tschetschenen gegen das Zarenreich (18. Jahrhundert bis 1859)* (Wiesbaden; Reichert, 2007).

6. Michael Kemper, "The North Caucasian Khalidiyya and 'Muridism': Historiographical Problems," *Journal for the History of Sufism* 5 (2006): 111–26; Shamil Shikhaliev, "Sufii i rossiiskaia vlast' v Dagestane v 19-om – pervoi polovine 20-ogo veka: istoriia vzaimootnoshenii," *Obychnoe pravo i pravovoi pliuralizm na Kavkaze v XIX – nachale XX veka* (Karachaevsk: n.p., 2009), 294–302.

7. Michael Kemper, "Khālidiyya Networks in Dagestan and the Question of *Jihād*," *Die Welt des Islams* 42, no. 1 (2002): 41–71.

8. Shamil Shikhaliev, "Ustaz trekh tarikatov: Saifulla-kadi Bashlarov," *Dagestanskie sviatyni*, vol. 1, ed. by Amri R. Shikhsaidov (Makhachkala: Ėpokha, 2007), 146–64.

9. Kemper, "Khālidiyya Networks."

10. Shamil' Shikhaliev, "Bashlarov," *Bol'shaia rossiiskaia entsiklopediia* vol. 4 (Moscow: Bol'shaia rossiĭskaia ėntsiklopediia, 2006), 146; idem, "Saipulla-kadi," *Islam na territorii byvshei Rossiiskoi imperii: entsiklopedicheskii slovar'*, ed. by Stanislav M. Prozorov, fascicle 4 (Moscow: Izdatel'skaia firma "Vostochnaia lit-ra" RAN, 2003), 72–73.

11. Later renamed Sovetskii, today Shamil'skii *raion*.

12. Shamil' Shikhaliev, "Iz istorii poiavleniia v Dagestane posledovatelei nakshbandiiskogo in shaziliiskogo tarikatov," *Gosudarstvo i religiia v Dagestane: Informationno-analiticheskii biulleten'* no. 1 (4) (Makhachkala: Izd. Dagpress, 2003), 39–57; idem, "Sufiiskie seti Dagestana: rasprostranenie i mezhregional'noe sotrudnichestvo," *Islam v sovremennom mire: vnutrikonfessional'nyi i mezhdunarodnyi-politicheskii aspekty. Ezhekvartal'nyi al'manakh* 7 (2007): 154–58 [I'm treating this as a journal]; I.Kh. Sulaev, *Gosudarstvo i musul'manskoe dukhovenstvo v Dagestane: istoriia vzaimootnoshenii (1917–1991)* (Makhachkala: [s.n.], 1991), 103–28.

13. Shamil Shikhaliev, "Downward Mobility and Spiritual Life: The Development of Sufism in the Context of Migrations in Dagestan, 1940s–2000s," in *Allah's Kolkhozes: Migration, De-Stalinisation, Privatisation and the New Muslim Congregations in the Soviet Realm (1950s–2000s)*, ed. by Stéphane A. Dudoignon and Christian Noack (Berlin: Klaus Schwarz, 2014), 412–14.

14. Moshe Gammer, "From the Challenge of Nationalism to the Challenge of Islam: The Case of Daghestan," in *Ethno-Nationalism, Islam and the State in the Caucasus: Post-Soviet Disorder*, ed. by Moshe Gammer (London; New York: Routledge, 2008), 182–84.

15. For a chronology of the events, see the section "Epilogue: The Split of DUMSK and the Split of DUMD," in Michael Kemper and Shamil Shikhaliev, "Administrative Islam: Two Soviet Fatwas from the North Caucasus," in *Islamic Authority and the Russian Language*, 99–102.
16. Gammer, "From the Challenge of Nationalism to the Challenge of Islam," 185–87.
17. [Akhmad-khadzhi Abdulaev], *Muftii Dagestana (propovedi, vystupleniia, interv'iu)* (Makhachkala: Biblioteka "Risalat," Seriia Irsilal, 2010),"," 46.
18. Dmitrii V. Makarov, *Ofitsial'nyi i neofitsial'nyi islam v Dagestane* (Moscow: TSentr strategicheskikh i politicheskikh issledovaniĭ, 2000).
19. For a first overview of Islamic institutes in Daghestan see Vladimir Bobrovnikov, Amir Navruzov, and Shamil Shikhaliev, "Islamic Education in Soviet and Post-Soviet Daghestan," *Islamic Education in the Soviet Union and Its Successor States*, ed. by Michael Kemper, Raoul Motika, and Stefan Reichmuth (London: Routledge, 2009), 151–59.
20. For cases see Matsuzato and Ibragimov, "Islamic Politics."
21. Kaflan M. Khanbabaev, "DUMD v usloviiakh modernizatsii dagestanskogo obshchestva," *Traditsionalizm i modernizatsiia na Severnom Kavkaze: vozmozhnost'i granitsy sovmestimosti*, ed. by V.V. Chernous, special issue of *Iuzhnorossiiskoe obozrenie TsSRIP IPPK RGU i ISPI RAN* 23 (2004), 163–92.
22. A few of his *murid*s continued to follow Arslanali Gamzatov as their shaykh, on the basis of a second Shadhiliyya license that he had apparently obtained from another shaykh of that brotherhood from Arabia. Still, Arslanali remained a loyal follower of Said-Afandi.
23. Fieldwork by Shamil Shikhaliev, August 2011: interviews with several *murid*s of Said-Afandi.
24. See the Shadhiliyya *silsila* published on the back cover of Magomed A. Amirkhanov's publication *Sheikh Shazili (Qutbu ghavs Abu Khasan Ali ash-Shazili)* (Makhachkala, s.n.s., 2002), where several non-Avars (still including Gamzatov) are included in the spiritual line of the local Shadhiliyya. In the Mahmudiyya, the only non-Avar shaykh is the Dargin Abdulvakhid-Afandi Kurbangadzhiev (b. 1933) from the village of Kakamakhi (Levashinskii *raion*). Malamukhammad-Afandi al-Zakatali, working in northern Azerbaijan (where there are more Lezgis than Avars among the Daghestani population) is an ethnic Avar.
25. Alexander Knysh, "Islam and Arabic as the Rhetoric of Insurgency: The Case of the Caucasus Emirate," *Studies in Conflict and Terrorism* 35 (2012): 315–37.
26. Kevin Daniel Leahy, "From Racketeer to Emir: A Political Portrait of Russia's Most Wanted Man," *Caucasus Review of International Affairs* 4, no. 3 (Summer 2010): 248–70.
27. For a general introduction into the political system and the state's policies towards radicalism, see Robert Bruce Ware and Enver Kisriev, *Dagestan: Russian Hegemony and Islamic Resistance in the Caucasus* (Armonk NY and London: M.E. Sharpe, 2010); Z.M. Abdulagatov, *Islam v massovom soznanii dagestantsev* (Makhachkala: [IIAE DNTS RAN], 2008); Akhmet Yarlykapov, "The Radicalization of North Caucasian

ISLAM AND POLITICAL VIOLENCE IN POST-SOVIET DAGHESTAN   149

Muslims," *Russia and Islam: State, Society, and Radicalism*, ed. by Roland Dannreuther and Luke March (London: Routledge, 2010), 137–54; Akhmet A. Iarlykapov, "Severokavkazskie molodezhnye dzhamaaty," *Novye etnicheskie gruppy v Rossii: puti grazhdanskoi integratsii*, ed. by V.V. Stepanov and V.A. Tishkov (Moscow: Institut etnologii i antropologii RAN, 2008), 346–50.

28. Interview of Shamil Shikhaliev with the Dargin theologian Kalimulla Gadzhiev (b. 1958), imam of the mosque in Kaspiisk (June 2003).

29. Fieldwork by Shamil Shaikhaliev, 2010–12 (interviews with several graduates of Syrian Islamic universities in Khasaviurt); as well as information from social media (Facebook, "Islamskaia tsivilizatsiia" [http://islamcivil.ru], and others).

30. *Respublika Dagestan. Zakon o zaprete vakhkhabitskoi i inoi ekstremistskoi deiatel'nosti na territorii Respubliki Dagestan.* 22 Sept. 1999, No. 15 (several additions were made in 2004 and 2007). The 1999 law banned "Wahhabi and other extremist" activities, including religious missions from abroad and individual missionaries, but also the production and possession of related literature. An addition from 2004 stipulates that Daghestani citizens are not allowed to study at religious teaching institutes outside of the Russian Federation except "if sent by the administrative organ in charge of the republican religious organizations [that is, DUMD], in accordance with the state organ for religious affairs of the Daghestan Republic [that is, the Committee for Religious Affairs]."

31. Abuzagir Arzulumovich Mantaev, "'Vakhkhabizm' i politicheskaia situatsiia v Dagestane," (PhD diss, Diplomatic Academy of the Russian Foreign Ministry 2012); idem, "Sufizm i vakhkhabizm v Dagestane v kontse 19 – nachale 20 vv.," *Islamskaia tsivilizatsiia* (Makhachkala), 1/2005, 43–46; Iasin (Makhach) Rasulov, "Kontseptual'naia priroda shariata," *Islamskaia tsivilizatsiia* 1/2005, 9–12; idem, *Dzhikhad na Severnom Kavkaze: storonniki i protivniki* (78 pages, without date and place, available on various websites). In 2005 both Mantaev and Iasulov were killed in the course of anti-terrorist operations (9 and 25 October, respectively), and several of the above-mentioned publications have officially been banned in the Russian Federation (mostly by provincial courts in the context of cases where suspects had these publications at home).

32. The history of Jadidism in Daghestan is only beginning to be studied. By contrast to Crimean and Volga Tatar Jadidism (from which the Daghestani Jadids certainly took their models), Daghestani Jadidism was from the onset multinational and multilingual; and while, like in Tatar Jadidism, the use of vernacular languages was important also to the Jadids in Daghestan, the latter also continued to use Arabic, the traditional Daghestani lingua franca for inter-ethnic written communication. Even the major Jadid newspapers were in Arabic; see Amir R. Navruzov, *"Dzharidat Dagistan" – araboiazychnaia gazeta kavkazskikh dzhadidov* (Moscow: Mardzhani, 2012). For a general characterization of Jadidism in Daghestan, see Shamil Shikhaliev and Michael Kemper, "Qadimism and Jadidism in Twentieth-century Daghestan", *Asiatische Studien – Études Asiatiques*, vol. 69, issue 3 (fall 2015).

33. Various anti-Sufi writings of the above-mentioned Jadidi authors are kept in the manuscript collection of the Institute of History, Archaeology and Ethnography of the Daghestani Center of the Russian Academy of Sciences in Makhachkala. For Muhammad

'Umari al-Ukhli, see Shamil' Shikhaliev, "'Al-Dzhavab as-salikh li-l-akh al-musallakh' 'Abd al-Khafiza Okhlinskogo," *Dagestan i musul'manskii vostok: sbornik statei*, ed. A.K. Alikberov and V.O. Bobrovnikov (Moscow: publisher?, 2010), 324–40. On Kaiaev and Saidov see Michael Kemper, *"Ijtihad* into Philosophy: Islam as Cultural Heritage in Post-Stalinist Daghestan," *Central Asian Survey* 33, no. 3 (2014): 390–404.

34. Cf. Dewin DeWeese, "Survival Strategies: Reflections on the Notion of Religious 'Survivals' in Soviet Ethnographic Studies of Muslim Religious Life in Central Asia," *Exploring the Edge of Empire: Soviet Era Anthropology in the Caucasus and Central Asia*, ed. by Florian Mühlfried and Sergey Sokolovskiy (Münster: Lit, 2011), 35–58.

35. See Muhammad al-Ya'subi al-'Asawi, *al-Ajwiba al-wahhabiyya 'ala al-masa'il al-wahmiyya*, Arabic manuscript (36 folios); and idem, *Ajwibat al-Ya'sub al-'Asali li-turrahat al-Wahhabi al-Harakani* (35 fols), a response to al-Harakani's attacks on Sufism. The latter manuscript copy dates from 1381/1962, documenting that the debate was still alive in the "middle" Soviet period. Manuscripts in private possession; digital copies in possession of Shamil Shikhaliev.

36. Zayni Dahlan's *Fitnat al-Wahhabiyya* has been published repeatedly in Russian translation; see, for instance, *Muftii goroda Mekka As-Saiid Akhmad Zeinii Dakhlian. Zabluzhdenie Vahhabistov. Fitnat al-Wahhabiyya* (Kiev: Otdel Issledovanii i perevodov Islamskogo Universiteta pri Dukhovnom upravlenii musul'man Ukrainy, 1998).

37. Sheikh Said-Afandi al'-Chirkavi, *Sokrovishchina blagodatnykh znanii – Majmu'at al-fawa'id* (Makhachkala: "Ikhlas"," 2002), 11.

38. Kuramukhammad-khadzhi Ramazanov, *Ostorozhno Vakhkhabizm!* (Makhachkala: DUMD, 2007), part one, 4. This brochure (in two fascicles) is based on Ramazanov's more comprehensive book *Zabluzhdenie vakhkhabizma v shariatskikh voprosov* (Makhachkala: n.p., 2007).

39. Ramazanov, *Ostorozhno Vakhkhabizm!* part one, 4–8.

40. Herein Ramazanov follows the anti-Jadid (anti-"Wahhabi") argumentation of Mahmudiyya shaykh Muhammad Ya'sub al-'Asali (d. 1942), without acknowledgment.

41. Ramazanov, *Ostorozhno Vakhkhabizm!*, (Makhachkala: DUMD,, 2007), part two, 4.

42. Ibid., 20.

43. Ramazanov, *Ostorozhno Vakhkhabizm!* part one, 10 and 16.

44. *Komu bylo vygodno poiavlenie vakhkhabizma. Priznanie angliiskogo shpiona*, supposedly translated from the Arabic [which is nonsense—it must have been translated from a Turkish edition from Hakikat Kitabevi, Istanbul] by R.G. Gadzhiev (Makhachkala: "Iupiter", 2000). For an English translation of these "Confessions of a British Spy" see http://www.hakikatkitabevi.com/download/english/14-ConfessionsOf%20ABritish-Spy.pdf. For its debunking see http://en.wikipedia.org/wiki/Memoirs_of_Mr._Hempher,_The_British_Spy_to_the_Middle_East .

45. Ramazanov, *Ostorozhno Vakhkhabizm!*, part one, 17.

46. Magomedrasul Omarov, *Alim Kuramukhammad-khadzhi* (Makhachkala: "Risalat", 2010), 41–42.

47. Abdulaev, *Muftii Dagestana*, 143–44.
48. Omarov, *Alim Kuramukhammad-khadzhi*, 9–23. Said-Afandi wrote his poem in Avar. The 2010 publication gives a literal Russian translation that has little aesthetic value because it does not rhyme.
49. Islam M. Aiubov, *Sufizm i litso Vakhkhabitov* (Makhachkala: DUMD & Institut IAE DNTs RAN 2010), 415 pages.
50. When asked by Kemper, a member of the Institute's Scientific Council (where all publications of the Institute are discussed) replied that he had not even heard about it.
51. Ruslan Magomedov, "Povyshenie muftiia," *Chernovik* (Makhachkala), No. 46 (23 November) 2012; http://chernovik.net/content/novosti/povyshenie-muftiya
52. Akhmad-khadzhi Abdulaev, *Muftii Dagestana*, 11–17 (a speech given at a meeting of the Anti-Terrorism Commission of the Republic Dagestan, not dated).
53. Abdulaev, *Muftii Dagestana*, 184, with reference to the well-known sociologist Dr. Enver Kisriev (Moscow). Abdulaev attacks Kisriev for the latter's advice to abolish the anti-Wahhabi law in Daghestan.
54. Patimat Gamzatova, "'Khudaibiiskii' 'mirnyi' dogovor," *islam.ru: islamskii informatsionnyi portal*, 2 September 2012; http://www.islam.ru/content/analitics/5140
55. "Rezoliutsiia po itogam sovmestnoi vstrechi Assotsiatsii uchenykh akhliu-sunny v Dagestane i Dukhovnogo upravleniia musul'man Dagestana," *Kavkazskii Uzel* 8 May 2012; http://www.kavkaz-uzel.ru/articles/206244/
56. Said-Afandi himself gives the following spiritual chain of the Mahmudiyya line that he represented: Mahmud Afandi al-Almali (1808–77) – Jabra'il Afandi – 'Abdarrahman al-'Asawi (1834–1905) – Hasan Afandi al-Qahi (1852–1937) – Muhammad Ya'sub al-'Asali (1886–1942) – Humayd Afandi al-Andikhi (1868–1952) – Muhammad Husayn al-Uribi (1862–1967) – Muhammad 'Arif al-Qahi (1900–1977) – Muhammad Saaduha-jji from Batlukh (1915–95) – 'Abdulhamid Afandi from Verkhnee Inkho (1888–1977) – Hamzat Afandi from Tliakh (1892–1985) – Muhammad Afandi from Khuchada (1909–87) – Badruddin Afandi from Botlikh (1913–95) – Sa'id Afandi Chirkevi (1937–2012). The diagram also contains a direct line from Muhammad Afandi Khuchadi to Sa'id Afandi Chirkevi, so that Said-Afandi is also presented as having a diploma from the shaykh of his direct shaykh, Badruddin-Afandi. See Sheikh Said-Afandi al'-Chirkavi, *Sokrovishchina blagodatnykh znanii – Majmu'at al-fawa'id* (Makhachkala: Ikhlas, 2002), 223ff. (years added from other sources).
57. E.g. Chikasa Sa'id Afandi, *Mazhmu'atul' Favaid (Sualal-zhavabal)* (s.l., n.p., 2000), which came out three years later in Russian (the above mentioned title *Sokrovishchina blagodatnykh znanii*).
58. Hasan Hilmi ibn Muhammad al-Qahi, *Talkhis al-ma'arif fi targhib Muhammad-'Arif* (1996); idem, *al-Buruj al-mushayyada bi l-nusus al-mu'ayyada* (1996); idem, *Tanbih al-salikin ila ghurur al-mutashayyikhin* (1996); idem, *Maktubat al-Qahi al-musamma Wasa'il al-murid fi rasa'il al-ustadh al-farid* (1998); idem, *al-Sifr al-asna fi l-rabita al-husna* (1998); as well as Mir Khalid Sayfallah b. Husayn Bashlar al-Nitsubkri al-Ghazi-Ghumuqi al-Daghistani, *Maktubat Khalid Sayfallah ila fuqara' ahl Allah* (1998).

All of these Arabic editions came out in Damascus in the Dar al-Nu'man li l-'ulum publishing house, with a certain 'Abd al-Jalil al-'Ata al-Bakri signing as editor.

59. Shu'ayb b. Idris al-Bagini, *Tabaqat al-khwajagan al-naqshbandiyya*, ed. by 'Abd al-Jalil al-'Ata al-Bakri (Damascus: Dar al-Nu'man li l-'ulum, 1417/1996). A 1999 re-edition has as an appendix another important Khalidiyya work written by the Tatar shaykh Muhammad ibn 'Abd al-Wahhab al-Chistawi, *Tabsirat al-murshidin min al-mashayikh al-khalidiyin* (with separate pagination).

60. For an overview see Shamil' Shikhaliev, "Dagestanskaia sufiiskaia literatura v XIX – nachale XX v. Kratkii obzor," *Pax Islamica – Mir Islama* (Moscow), 2 (2009), 63–89.

61. Sheikh Khasan Khil'mi ibn Mukhammad al-Dagestani an-Nakshbandi al-Shazili al-Kadiri, *Talkhis al'-ma'ariffi targib Mukhammad 'Arif. Kratkoe izlozhenie sokrovennykh znanii dlia nastavleniia Mukhammada 'Arifa*, transl. from the Arabic by I.R. Nasyrov and A.S. Atsaev (Moscow: "Islam", 2006).

62. Sheikh Khasan Khil'mi Afandi, *Khulasat-ul'-adab: sushchnost' etiki dlia zhelaiushchikh otkryt' vrata poznaniia Allakha* (Makhachkala: publisher?; first ed. 1999, fourth ed. 2010).

63. Qahisa Hasan Afandi, *Siraju sa'adat* (Makhachkala: s.n.s., 2001). A different Avar booklet under the same title (Makhachkala: Nur-ul Islam, 2001) seems to be based on Bagini's Mahmudiyya biographies/hagiographies, and cannot be (completely) assigned to Hasan al-Qahi. See Shamil' Shikhaliev, "Sochinenie Khasana Khilmi al-Kakhi 'Siradzh as-Saadat': kratkii istoricheskii obzor," *Nauchnoe obozrenie: Ezhekvartal'nyi sbornik statei* (Makhachkala) 52 (2011): 4–11.

64. Magomed A. Amirkhanov, *Mir islama* (Makhachkala: s.n.., 1996).

65. M.A. Amirkhanov, *Shuaib Afandi al-Bagini. 155-letiiu nakshubandiiskogo sheikha, khafiza sviashchennogo qurana, 'alima-shafiita, mubaraka Shuaiba-khadzhi-afandi al-Bagini* (Makhachkala, n.p., 2007); M.A. Amirkhanov, *Ibragkhim-khadzhi-afandi al-Kuchri. 144-letiiu nakshubandiiskogo sheikha Ibrakhima-khadzhi-afandi al-Kuchri* (Makhachkala: n.p., 2007).

66. Mukhammad Gadzhiev, *Solntse nastavleniia. Sheikh Mukhammad-afandi. Ego nastavniki i preemniki* (Makhachkala: Nur-ul Islam, 2011).

67. For comparative material see Allen J. Frank, *Islamic Popular Literature in Kazakhstan: An Annotated Bibliography* (Hyattsville, MD: Dunwoody Press, 2007); and Stéphane A. Dudoignon, "Local Lore, the Transmission of Learning, and Communal Identity in Late 20th-century Tajikistan: The *Khujand-Nama* of 'Arifan Yahyazad Khujandi," *Devout Societies vs. Impious States? Transmitting Islamic Learning in Russia, Central Asia and China, through the Twentieth Century*, edited by Stéphane A. Dudoignon (Berlin: Schwarz, 2004), 213–42.

68. Jürgen Paul, "Hagiographische Texte als historische Quelle," *Saeculum: Jahrbuch für Universalgeschichte* 41, no. 1 (1990): 17–43.

69. See, e.g., Said-Afandi al'-Chirkavi, *Sbornik vystuplenii. Tom pervyi* (Makhachkala: Chirkeiskii institut im. Saida-Afandi – Severokavkazskii universitetskii tsentr islamskogo obrazovaniia i nauki; "Nurul' Irshad", 2010).

70. For an analysis of Bagini's description of miracles, see Shamil' Sh. Shikhaliev and Makhach A. Musaev, "Chudesnye deianiia sviatykh v araboiazychnykh sufiiskikh biograficheskikh sochineniiakh dagestanskikh sheikhov nachala XX veka," *Pis'mennye pamiatniki vostoka* 2 (17) (2012): 218–32.

71. A similar, even more comprehensive representative of the same individual genre is Rakhmatulla Magomedov's *Khamzat-afandi iz Tliakha* (Makhachkala: s.n., 2009). This book is a Russian translation from the Avar.

72. For an example see Patimat I. Takhnaeva, *Argvani: mir ushedshikh stoletii. Istoricheskii portret sel'skoi obshchiny Nagornogo Dagestana* (Moscow: Izdatel'skaia firma "Vostochnaia literatura", 2012), 301ff; Makhach A. Musaev, Patimat I. Takhnaeva, "Opyt issledovaniia biografii sufiiskikh sheikhov (na primere Abu-Bakra (Bulach-khana) al-Ingishi)," *Vestnik Maikopskogo gosudarstvennogoe tekhnologicheskogo universiteta* 2/2011: 40–45; Z.B. Ibragimova, "Obshchaia kharakteristika sochineniia v zhanre biografii sufiiskikh sheikhov 'Khikaia va manakib al-mashaikh an-nakshbandiia'", *Nauchnoe obozrenie: Ezhekvartal'nyi sbornik statei* (Makhachkala), no. 52 (2011): 12–14.

73. Mukhammad-khadzhi Abdurakhmanov, *Zolotaia tsepochka nakshbandiiskikh sheikhov* (Makhachkala: Ikhlas, 2004).

74. For this claim see Sheikh Said-Afandi al'-Chirkavi, *Sokrovishchina blagodatnykh znanii – Majmu'at al-fawa'id*, 223–51.

75. Magomedrasul Omarov (ed.), *Gorskaia mudrost'* (""Makhachkala: IATs "Fikr", 2009), inner cover page.

76. Omarov (ed.), *Gorskaia mudrost'*, 111–13.

77. Omarov (ed.), *Gorskaia mudrost'*, 104–6.

78. Gubdalan Abu Muslim, *Huni tariqat marhebirulriv?* [Russian title: "Ty ne priznaesh' tarikat?!"] (Makhachkala: Ikhlas, 2001); *Hasan Hilmi (1863–1937), Suleiman, Jamaluddin, Gubdalan Abu Muslim, tariqatla cherdek'ibti adabti (Khulasat al-adab)* (Makhachkala: Iupiter, [s.d.]).

79. Cf. Alexander Knysh, "A Clear and Present Danger: 'Wahhabism' as a Rhetorical Foil," *Die Welt des Islams* 44, no. 1 (2004): 3–26.

80 See, however, the Russian translation of an Arabic letter written by the Khalidiyya shaykh Mukhammad-Mukhtar Babatov (b. 1954): M.-M. Babatov, "Pis'mo Magomed-Mukhtara Paraul'skogo Magomedu, synu Ali Iordanskogo – prepodavateliu islamskikh nauk v s. Karamakhi Buinakskogo raiona. Perevod s arabskogo K.K. Khidirbekova," *Alimy i uchenye protiv vakhkhabizma* (Makhachkala: Dagestanskoe knizhnoe izdatel'stvo, 2001), 59–83. Also published were some brochures by the Khalidiyya shaykh Mukhadzhir Akaev (d. 2010) on issues of Islamic and Sufi ethics and a few biographies of shaykhs.

81. In addition to the examples mentioned in passim (Abdulzhalil, his disciple Gadzhiev, and Mukhammad Abdurakhmanov, author of the *Golden Chain*), the former DUMD Mufti (and disciple of Said-Afandi) Saiidmukhammad-Hajji Abubakarov (d. 1998) also had an educational background in medicine, as does Abubakarov's father, Khas-

Mukhammad Abubakarov. While not being a shaykh, Khas-Mukhammad Abubakarov is an influential person in both DUMD and the Mahmudiyya; he directs the S.-M. Abubakarov charitable foundation, named after his assassinated son.
82. Alfrid K. Bustanov, "Rafail' Valishin's 'Anti-Wahhabi' Sufi Traditionalism in Rural Western Siberia," in Bustanov and Kemper, *Islamic Authority and the Russian Language*, 219–63.

About the Editor and Contributors

MICHAEL KEMPER is professor of Eastern European Studies at the University of Amsterdam. His field of research is Islam in Russia, especially in the Volga Urals and the North Caucasus, on the basis of Arabic and Turkic manuscripts. In recent international projects he has explored the history of Oriental Studies in the USSR (*Reassessing Orientalism: Interlocking Orientologies during the Cold War*, edited by M. Kemper and A.M. Kalinovsky, Routledge, 2015), and the emergence of Islamic variants of the Russian language (*Islamic Authority and the Russian Language: Studies on Texts from European Russia, the North Caucasus and West Siberia*, ed. A.K. Bustanov and M. Kemper, Amsterdam: Pegasus 2012).

HIROTAKE MAEDA is Associate Professor of History at Tokyo Metropolitan University. His main publications are: "On the Ethno-Social Background of the Four *Gholām* Families from Georgia in Safavid Iran", *Studia Iranica* Tome 32, 2003; "Parsadan Gorgijanidze's Exile in Shushtar", *Journal of Persianate Studies*, Volume 1, Number 2, 2008; "The Household of Allāhverdī Khān: An Example of Patronage Network in Safavid Iran", Florence Hellot-Bellier and Irène Natchkebia eds., *La Géorgie entre Perse et Europe*, Paris: l'Harmattan, 2009; "Slave Elites Who Returned Home: Georgian *Vālī*-king Rostom and the Safavid Household Empire," *Memoirs of the Research Department of the Toyo Bunko*, 69 (2011); "Exploitation of the Frontier: The Caucasus Policy of Shah 'Abbas I," Willem Floor and Edmund Herzig (eds.), *Iran and the World in the Safavid Age*, London: I. B. Tauris 2012.

SEAN POLLOCK received his PhD in History from Harvard University and is Associate Professor of History and Faculty Director of the Center for Teaching and Learning at Wright State University. He is currently working on a study of the life and "afterlives" of Prince Petr Ivanovich Bagration (1765–1812).

MICHAEL A. REYNOLDS is Associate Professor of Near Eastern Studies at Princeton University. He is the author of *Shattering Empires: The Clash and Collapse of the Ottoman-Russian Empires, 1908–1918* (Cambridge University Press, 2011) a recipient of the American Historical Association's George Louis Beer Prize.

SHAMIL SHIKHALIEV is senior coworker at the Institute of History, Archeology and Ethnography, Russian Academy of Sciences, Makhachkala. He has published widely on the history of Sufism and of Jadidism in Daghestan, for which he explores private Muslim libraries in the mountains. Among his recent publications is "Downward Mobility and Spiritual Life: The Development of Sufism in the Context of Migrations in Dagestan, 1940s–2000s," in *Allah's Kolkhozes: Migration, De-Stalinisation, Privatisation and the New Muslim Congregations in the Soviet Realm (1950s–2000s)*, ed. by St. A. Dudoignon and Chr. Noack (Berlin: Klaus Schwarz, 2014), 398–420.

RONALD GRIGOR SUNY is Wiliam H. Sewell Distinguished University Professor of History at the University of Michigan and Emeritus Professor of Political Science and History at the University of Chicago. He is author of *The Baku Commune, 1917–1918*; *The Making of the Georgian Nation*; *Looking Toward Ararat: Armenia in Modern History*; *The Revenge of the Past: Nationalism, Revolution, and the Collapse of the Soviet Union*; *The Soviet Experiment: Russia, the USSR, and the Successor States*; *"They Can Live in the Desert But Nowhere Else": A History of the Armenian Genocide*; and co-editor of *A Question of Genocide: Armenians and Turks at the End of the Ottoman Empire*.

PRINCETON SERIES ON THE MIDDLE EAST

Cyrus Schayegh and William Blair, Editors
Department of Near Eastern Studies, Princeton University

Al-Jabartī's History of Egypt
edited with an introduction and commentary
by Jane Hathaway
   "The most accessible and comprehensive primary source for the history of Egypt under Ottoman rule."
   —*Book News*
HC 978-1-55876-446-0   PB 978-1-55876-447-7

The Book of Strangers: Medieval Arabic Graffiti on the Theme of Nostalgia
edited and translated by Patricia Crone and Smuel Moreh.
   "An exemplary translation... readable and well documented"—*TLS*
HC 978-1-55876-214-5   PB 978-1-55876-233-6

Harem Ghosts: What One Cemetery Can Tell Us about the Ottoman Empire
by Douglas Scott Brookes and Ali Ziyrek
HC 978-1-55876-610-5   PB 978-1-55876-611-2

The Heritage of Central Asia:
From Antiquity to the Turkish Expansion
by Richard N. Frye
   "A handy book. ... Frye surveys the true history ... beautiful."—*Washington Post*
   "Incontestably one of the best studies of the history of Central Asia."—*Journal of Indo-European Studies*
   "Outstanding academic book of the year"—*Choice*
HC 978-1-55876-110-0   PB 978-1-55876111-7

PRINCETON SERIES ON THE MIDDLE EAST
(continued)

Jihad – A History in Documents
by Rudolph Peters
(updated and expanded 2016 edition)
  "A handy reader"—*Journal of Near Eastern Studies*
  "Enlightening"—*Journal for World History*
HC 978-1-55876-608-2   PB 978-1-55876-609-9

The Levant: A Fractured Mosaic
by William Harris
(updated and expanded 2015 edition)
  "A well researched and engaging book"—*Library Journal*
HC 978-1-55876-602-0   PB 978-1-55876-603-7

The Middle Eastern Economy: Decline and Recovery
by Charles Issawi
  "Gracefully written, filled with historical insight. ...
  A pleasure to read."—*Foreign Affairs*
HC 978-1-55876-102-5   PB 978-1-55876-103-2

New Faces of Lebanon
by William Harris
  "An excellent book, well written and documented"
  —*Library Journal*
HC 978-1-55876-391-3   PB 978-1-55876-392-0

The Saudi Kingdom Between Jihadi Hammer and Iranian Anvil
by Ali Al Shihabi; preface by Bernard Haykel
HC 978-1-55876-612-9   PB 978-1-55876-613-6

PRINCETON SERIES OF MIDDLE EASTERN SOURCES IN TRANSLATION

General Editor, M. Şükrü Hanioğlu

The Arabs: A Short History
by Heinz Halm
Expanded edition with documents selected and edited
  by Luke Yarbrough and Oded Zinger
HC 978-1-55876-545-0   PB 978-1-55876-546-7

Modern Iran: A History in Documents
Edited translated and introduced by Negin Nabavi
HC 978-1-55876-600-6   PB 978-1-55876-601-3

The History by of Maritime Wars of the Turks
by Çelebi, Kâtip
edited and annotated by Svatopluk Soucek)
HC 978-1-055876-547-4   PB 978-1-055876-548-1

www.ingramcontent.com/pod-product-compliance
Lightning Source LLC
Chambersburg PA
CBHW020949230426
43666CB00005B/244